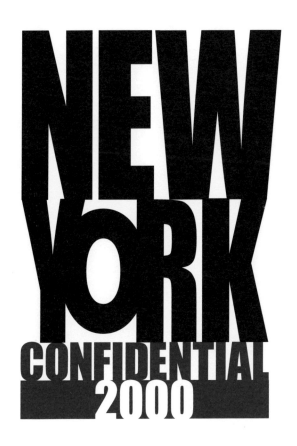

NEW YORK CONFIDENTIAL 2000

ASSOULINE

© Assouline Publishing
601 West 26th Street, New York, NY 10001
Tel: 212-989-6810   Fax: 212-647-0005
www.assouline.com

English Translation by Holly Warner © Assouline, 1999

Distributed in North America by St. Martin's Press.

Distributed in Canada by McClelland Stewart.

Distributed in all other countries, excluding North America and
Canada, by Thames and Hudson Distributors, Ltd.

ISBN : 2 84323 173 6

Printed in Italy

Camille Labro and Stéphanie Chayet

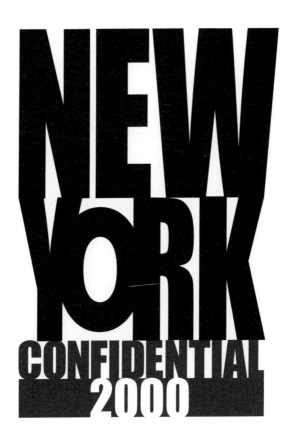

NEW YORK CONFIDENTIAL 2000

ASSOULINE

NEW YORK CONFIDENTIAL 2000

Foreword

You've done the Met, Tiffany's and the Empire State Building. You know all about exchange rates, and you've got tipping down pat. These basics won't be covered in this guide.

Instead we'll lead you off the beaten track, so you can discover for yourself the New Yorker's New York. In these pages, you'll find a subjective but scrupulous selection of the most chic, innovative, unusual and avant-garde places that New York has to offer. And, because you're not here just to satisfy your vital needs (eating, drinking and sleeping), we've also included other New York essentials: bridges, beaches, boats, gardens, hairdressers, swimming pools, marketplaces, dance lessons and art galleries, old movie houses and boutiques....

Finally, because we believe you get the most out of a city when you live at its rhythm and in sync with its moods, we've added a few "keys" to the current trends that make this metropolis vibrate—from Mambo to Illbient, from boxing to bowling... You'll discover the latest cocktails, the newest young designers and the best vintage furniture stores. You'll know where to listen to underground DJs, dance beneath the stars, dine in Brooklyn or watch Shakespeare in a park.

Neophyte or old hand, here for a weekend or forever, you'll discover another New York in these pages, a confidential New York.

Camille Labro and Stéphanie Chayet

Note: New York is an ever-changing city, so we apologize in advance if some of these addresses are outdated by the time you get to them. Of course, those changes are part of what make this such an exciting place!

Rooms]

According to the latest statistics, New York has 65,000 hotel rooms. We've visited dozens of them, in every style and price range, paying more attention to atmosphere, charm and details than to reputations. Our suggestions will fulfill diverse lodging needs. Like we were told by the owner of *Bevy's Soho Loft*: "There are hotel people and bed & breakfast people, those who love being anonymous and surrounded by comfort, and those who are looking for a warm, personal environment." Whether you prefer big hotel lobbies peopled with jet-setters, small, colorful family guesthouses or tiny brick walk-ups, whether you need a suite with room-service or a cozy attic in the Village, our choices offer, in our opinion, the best in their categories.

ABINGDON GUEST HOUSE / Discreet sophistication
13 8th Ave. & W. 12th Street
Tel.: (212) 243-5384
Fax: (212) 807-7473
www.abingdonguesthouse.com

It took us three years to realize that the small café where we bought our bagels every morning was the ground floor of a very classy guesthouse—with good reason: Abingdon Guest House has no sign. The door, in the vestibule of the Brewbar Coffee Bar, looks like the entry to a private building, and it's in this café where clients get their keys and pay their bills. But once you've climbed the narrow staircase, you'll find immaculate rooms elegantly decorated in dark colors and filled with "Old England" style furniture. All nine rooms are named for an aristocrat (Windsor, Roxbury, Polo, Landau, Ambassador). Each has its own private phone line with an answering machine, cable TV, and most have a private bath. The prices are a bargain ($80 to $200 a night with a four-night minimum), especially when you consider the quality, serenity and absolute discretion of the place.

BEVY'S SOHO LOFT / Artsy B&B
Mercer Street (address not specified at owner's request)
Tel.: (212) 431-8214
Fax: (212) 343-0218
www.sohobevy.com

For those who want to feel "at home" in New York, Bevy's picturesque duplex loft in the heart of Soho is the place. The septuagenarian lady of the house is as sparkly and fun as the decor of knick knacks, odds and ends she's spent the last fifteen years perfecting. The furniture was all bought in flea markets or found on the street, and the staircase is painted à la Frank Lloyd Wright. As for the odd-ball collection of sculptures and paintings that decorate the space, most are gifts from her clients. "My guests and I are like a big family—and I'm the Mom," she brags while rearranging a huge bouquet of tulips. With her bohemian sense of humor and creative energy, Bevy has written a movie script that recounts the thousands of stories of her B&B that you can read on her website. Each of the three rooms—of which two share the same bath—are spacious, comfortable and personalized and can be rented either by the day ($145 - $175) or by the month (between $1,200 and $2,500). Reservations by fax or internet.

Chapter 1

CARLTON ARMS / *Youth hostel with a twist*
160 E. 25th St., between Lexington & 3rd Ave.
Tel.: (212) 679-0680
www.hotwired/gallery/96/04/carlton.html

With its boisterous colors and weird decor, the *Carlton Arms* is one of New York's most curious, most bohemian and most underground hotels. It's also probably one of the best deals: $62 to $76 for a room with private bath, or $52 to $66 without (there are showers on every floor). A multicolored staircase swarming with visitors from the four corners of the world serves as a lobby, where Ty Inwood, the manager, welcomes everybody with an astounding placidity. As for the rooms, each has been decorated by a different artist. There's the stuffed animal room, the Love Nest (entirely draped in red chiffon), the Saloon with its bar counter and green lampshades, the Cartoon room, the Greek Antique room, the Boudoir, etc. Comfort is minimal (no phones, TV or toilets in the rooms), but if you're a bit of a rolling stone, this hotel (which is somewhere between Jack Kerouac, the B-52s and Fellini) will quickly become your favorite place to crash in New York.

INCENTRA VILLAGE HOUSE / *Country guesthouse*
32 8th Ave., between 12th & Jane St.
Tel.: (212) 206-0007
Fax: (212) 604-0625

Knowing how rare and precious a good downtown hotel is, we've included this one even though it is practically across the street from the *Abingdon Guest House*. Discreet and unpretentious, this favorite of the gay community has a friendly rural feel about it, almost like spending the weekend at a friend's country home. Guests are invited to tickle the ivories of the concert grand piano dominating the classically decorated living room. Among the ten small rooms (between $99 and $170), ask for one that overlooks the charming and delicious little garden, a world away from the city.

INN AT IRVING PLACE / *Quiet sumptuousness*
56 Irving Place & 17th St.
Tel.: (212) 533-4600
Fax: (212) 533-4611
www.innatirving.com

Models, photographers and scriptwriters looking for a refuge from the uptown turmoil have taken to hiding out behind the discreet facade of this 1830s house, two blocks from Gramercy Park. The owner, Naomi

Blumenthal, spent three years choosing the antique furnishings for her Victorian-style hotel. The result is utterly charming—from the sumptuous tearoom with its mahogany floors to the Venetian blinds, it's like being transported to an Edith Wharton or Henry James novel. On the ground floor, a pretty lounge spins onto a bamboo-planted courtyard. We actually prefer the simple and delicate decor of the standard rooms. Rates: from $295 to $450 per night.

INN NEW YORK CITY / *Refined libations*
266 W. 71st. St. & West End Ave.
Tel.: (212) 580-1900
Fax: (212) 580-4437

If you're the kind of person who measures the quality of a hotel room by the size of its bathroom, don't miss the "Spa Suite" of the *Inn New York City*. This Upper West Side house has no sign on the door and boasts what is surely the largest and most sumptuous bathtub in the entire city. Deep and round, it reigns upon a decor of Persian carpets and antique tiles, marble-topped make-up tables and old barber chairs. The room that goes with it is just as beautiful, with Venetian blinds, blue tapestries and Bakelite phones. The owners Ruth and Elyn (mother-and-daughter and both interior decorators) tend to their guests' every whim with newspapers and magazines, fresh flowers, pastries brought in daily from *Zabar's,* Italian coffee and exotic mineral waters. Each of the four suites ($415 per night) is equipped like a small apartment. Please note: this delicately perfumed house is strictly No Smoking.

LARCHMONT BED & BREAKFAST / *Good deal*
27 W. 11th St., between 5th & 6th Ave.
Tel.: (212) 989-9333
Fax: (212) 989-9496

On a calm, residential Greenwich Village block, this small fifty-four-room hotel is one of the best deals in the city. The choice of furniture—rattan chairs and tables, flowered cushions and bed-spreads—is not the most tasteful, but the rooms (all equipped with TV, telephones and washbasins) are quiet, and above all, impeccably clean. Each floor has nine rooms that share two bathrooms and a small kitchen—the hotel provides slippers and a robe to circulate in the hallways. The price ($70 for a single, $110 for a double with a Queen-size bed) includes a continental breakfast.

MANSFIELD HOTEL / *Elegance and serenity*
12 W. 44th St. & 5th Ave.
Tel.: (212) 944-6050
Fax: (212) 764-4477
www.mansfieldhotel.com

Renovated a few years ago, this hotel built in 1906 is a peaceful haven of marble, dark wood and copper in the midst of midtown madness. Chic and comfortable, mixing neoclassicism and modern design, the *Mansfield* invites luxurious relaxation. Next to the reception area, the vast reading room with 1920s furniture and lots of books feels like a turn-of-the-century men's club. A cream, taupe and ebony palette has been used in the calm, simple rooms and spacious suites, and the original steel and glass elevator with its uniformed porter is a touch of elegance hard to come by in this day and age. $200 for standard rooms, $1,200 for a penthouse suite.

MERCER HOTEL / *Modern opulence*
99 Prince St. & Mercer St.
Tel.: (212) 966-6060; restaurant: (212) 966-5454
Fax: (212) 965-3838

This is the latest hideaway for stars on the move. Located in an old warehouse and decorated by Frenchman Christian Liaigre, this modern palace swims in immaculate elegance: linen sheets, huge marble bathrooms and dimly lit dressing rooms. In the cellar, lit by translucent paving stones, a hallmark of old Soho, you'll find *The Kitchen*, run by talented chef Jean-Georges Vongerichten and serving Asian-American-influenced Provencal dishes. Reserve several months in advance and request a room on the courtyard (quieter than those on the street). $300 to $1,800.

PARAMOUNT / *Ocean-liner in the city*
235 W. 46th St., between 7th & 8th Ave.
Tel.: (212) 764-5500
Fax: (212) 354-5237
www.hotelbook.com

If the *Paramount* is the most affordable of Ian Schrager's empire, it's also the warmest and least pretentious. For the price (from $145 per night), Philippe Starck fans will be overwhelmed. The 610 rooms are a bit small, but the *Paramount* has a great sense of humor, and its details will win you: conical sinks, red roses pinned on the walls, pyramids of scarlet apples in the gym, and the kids playroom decorated by Gary Pentar (mastermind of Pee Wee

Herman's Playhouse). We especially like the staircase of fluctuating colors and inclined mirrors that give weather reports. If they show "cold and raining," don't worry—you can always people-watch in the lobby. Eclectically decorated and furnished with Mark Newson's "chaises longues" and sculpted banquettes by Gaudi, you will want to laze about there for hours. Bonus: the latest issue of *Time Out* in each room and a well-stocked international news stand at the entrance.

PIERRE HOTEL / *"Grand hotel"*
5th Ave. & 61st St.
Tel.: (212) 838-8000
Fax: (212) 940-8109
www.fourseasons.com

Of all the luxury hotels in New York, we've given an honorable mention to the seamless classicism of the *Pierre Hotel*. With its long, hushed corridors, mahogany furniture, monumental bouquets of lilies everywhere and impeccable service, the *Pierre* is right out of the movies. Each deluxe room has a private desk, make-up table, couch and coffee table as well as fresh fruit, a cell phone and of course, today's issue of *The New York Times*. Mere mortals may find the rates exorbitant (about $400 per night for the simplest rooms, up to $5,000 for a suite); in that case, don't miss tea in the ground floor rotunda—a romantic spot for an afternoon tryst or to recuperate after a shopping spree on Fifth Avenue.

ROOMS TO LET / *Rustic charm*
83 Horatio St. & Washington St.
Tel.: (212) 675-5481
Fax: (212) 675-9432
www.citysearch.com/nyc/roomstolet

In a beautiful little brownstone on the edge of the Meat Market and just one block from the Hudson River, this B&B is a bit of the country in the heart of the city. In the summer, the living room opens on to a small flowered garden, where you can relax in a hammock with Petunia, one of the resident cats. The five rooms—plus a ground floor apartment ($2,300 per month)—still seem lived in by owner Marjorie Colt's family. Her own paintings and family portraits line the walls and the rooms are named after her kids. An ideal single is Amy's Room ($90), and for couples we recommend The Attic, a fabulous hodge-podge decorated in quilts, old books and antiques ($160). The ceilings are low but the room is big and comfortable with a kitchenette and private bathroom. The catch: the landlady is a bit moody, and breakfast is a couple of pieces of toast and coffee that you might have to re-heat yourself.

Chapter 1

SOHO GRAND / *Top models and goldfish*
310 W. Broadway, between Grand & Canal St.
Tel.: (212) 965-3000
Fax: (212) 965-3244
www.sohogrand.com

When the *Soho Grand* was launched in 1996, it had been more than a century since a new hotel had opened in Soho. That, combined with William Sofield's interior decor (the mastermind who designed all the latest Gucci stores in Europe) soon grabbed the attention of fashion's jet-setters. Set inside a former factory on West Broadway, the building is a living tribute to the neighborhood's industrial past with its steel, bronze, glass and brick architecture. The huge metal staircase suspended on cables is a landmark in itself. The rooms are decorated in masculine monochromes (tobacco, beige, smoky gray) and stocked with *Dean & Deluca* groceries, *Kiehl's* cosmetics, and the daily papers—including the unavoidable *Woman's Wear Daily* during Fashion Week. Since the owner also runs a pet-toy and accessory company, this is one of the most animal-friendly hotels in New York. Cats and dogs have their own room service: $10 for a bowl of dog food (!), $8 for toys. And if you left Fido or Tweety at home, the concierge will lend you a goldfish in a bowl to keep you company. Prices: from $334 to $534 a room, and from $1,099 to $1,499 for one of the four penthouses with private terrace.

TIME HOTEL / *Technicolor palace*
224 W. 49th St., between Broadway & 8th Ave.
Tel.: (212) 320-2900
Fax: (212) 245-2305

If you've had enough of the beige and gray color scheme of today's minimalist hotels, take heart! The *Time Hotel* will cheer you. The result of a collaboration between a New York nightlife guru (Vikram Chatwell) and a chic interior decorator (Adam Tihany), this new establishment invites its guests to "experience the multiple moods of a primary color." The 200 rooms explore color themes in reds, greens or blues with gusto— if you choose red, for example, be forewarned that you'll be served strawberries for breakfast (those who prefer blueberries will have to choose a blue room) and scarlet jelly beans before spraying yourself with RED, the kumquat-scented perfume created exclusively for the hotel by *Fresh* cosmetics (see Beauty chapter). And for spiritual nourishment, a copy of "The Primary Colors," an essay by Alexander Theroux, is on every bed-side table. Beyond this stylistic exercise, *Time* proposes all the services you expect in this range: a large collection of high-tech gadgets (Web TV, Bose radios and cell phones), the highly praised *Palladin* restaurant on the ground floor, and beautiful people in every room. Price: $250 to $1,100 per night.

HOTEL LOBBIES

There is nothing more elegant or romantic than a hotel lobby. Even if we did not select them for their rooms, these hotels are worth a detour simply to have a drink, grab a cup of coffee, read the paper or quietly watch the world go by.

ALGONQUIN
59 W. 44th St., between 5th & 6th Ave. **Tel.: (212) 840-6800**
It's at the large round table of the *Algonquin* that Dorothy Parker reigned and at which the *New Yorker* was conceived. With frosted glass windows, elegant leather armchairs and a dusky penumbra, the Rose Room is a haven for relaxation and hushed exchanges. Enjoy a peaceful lunch, sip a whiskey on the rocks, savor a cigar or talk business away from the crowds and brouhaha of the city.

MORGANS
237 Madison Ave. & 37th St. **Tel.: hotel (212) 686-0300 ; bar: 726-7600**
With sumptuous velvet drapes, antique chandeliers and the aroma of musk-scented incense, the bar at *Morgan's* has an aura of quiet decadence. Stars in search of anonymity take refuge here in the club armchairs, and those who want to be seen seat themselves at the long well-lit table that runs-diagonally across the room. An ideal spot for that Martini nightcap.

ROYALTON
44 W. 44th St., between 5th & 6th Ave. **Tel.: (212) 944-8844**
The lobby of the *Royalton*—the result of the first collaboration between hotel-owner Ian Schrager and Philippe Starck—is a voluptuous oasis richly carpeted in sensual colors. Nothing could be more chic than sipping a Citrus Martini (Absolut Lemon and Grand Marnier) engulfed in the deep white armchairs and watching the parade of celebrities—real and affected—strut toward the elevators and the restaurant. You will feel like a celebrity yourself just by being there. Don't miss the restrooms with their impressive smoked-glass sliding doors.

TABLES

Tables]

Let it be said once and for all: the food in New York is fantastic provided that you avoid the greasy spoons and thematic tourist traps that proliferate around Times Square. Culinary inventiveness has reached an exuberant high point in New York today. Reflecting the city's cosmopolitan nature, the latest trend of "fusion food" (mixing tastes from the four corners of the world) has conquered the most difficult gourmet palates. New York has never offered so many options for eating out. There are the latest hip spots, the high-end restaurants, the timeless classics. And all the rest: neighborhood eateries, bustling bistros, romantic gardens, family tables, Italian, Chinese, Japanese, Indian, South American... The places we've chosen, for their menus as well as their atmospheres, include a selection of all of these. Don't forget to reserve and remember that most restaurants are closed on Mondays. Bon appetit!

AQUAGRILL / *Oyster heaven*
210 Spring St. & 6th Ave.
Tel.: (212) 274-0505

If you like seafood, this is for you. Behind its charming "sea blue" facade, *Aquagrill* serves up an extraordinary choice of fresh shell fish. Fifty varieties of oysters from all over the world are shipped in daily, ranging from big and creamy to delicate and translucent. If you can't make up your mind between the Wellfleet, Belon or Malpeques, the waiter will happily serve you some of each. You should also try the "Soup of the Day"—we had an unforgettable garlic and crab soup—and any of the many fish specials: grilled, poached or sauteed. Around $40.

ASIA DE CUBA / *High fusion*
237 Madison Ave., between 37th & 38th St.
Tel.: (212) 726-7755

Centered around one long communal table (all the better to see and be seen), *Asia de Cuba* is a social theater like you can only find in New York. The opulent decor created by Philippe Starck framed by heavy, deep pleated white curtains, the unforgivingly beautiful waitresses weaving between the tables in long Chinese sheaths, and the psychedelic-colored cocktails create a languorous atmosphere. Although the food, an Asian-Cuban fusion, is esthetically pleasing, appearances can be misleading at times. But here, it is not what you eat that really matters. About $45.

BALTHAZAR / *Prestigious brasserie*
80 Spring St. & Crosby St.
Tel.: (212) 965-1414

The media frenzy surrounding *Balthazar* has finally let up, but this warm and spacious French brasserie is still filled to the brim every evening. With good reason: the ever-changing menu thought up by owner Keith McNally, and his two chefs Riad Nsar and Lee Hanson, remains sensational. Depending on the season, original creations such as a succulent casserole of purple artichokes, rabbit with fennel or grilled trout with lentils are added to classic bistro staples like escargots, coq au vin, steak with pepper sauce or seafood platters. The first time you go to *Balthazar* might be to see and be seen, but it's the food that will keep you coming back—we've never been disappointed. Around $45.

BONDST / *Electrifying sushi*
6 Bond St., between Broadway & Lafayette
Tel.: (212) 777-2500

The epitome of the latest trend in minimalist Asian-New-York-chic is this three-story Noho restaurant. On the first two floors, the beautiful people crush together to sample melt-in-the-mouth sushi, airy tempuras and other high-flying creations by Hiroshi Nakahara and Linda Rodriguez (a former chef at *Nobu*). Warm, amber lighting, tatamis and Zen bouquets set the mood for an exquisite Japanese meal. In the bar downstairs, you'll have to push your way through a swarm of hip yuppies to sip the latest fashionable cocktail: the Saketini (martini with saké). About $45.

BOP / *Korean barbecue*
325 Bowery & 2nd St.
Tel.: (212) 254-7887

A simple decor of ideograms painted on the walls, a huge Chinese abacus and translucent screens bestow a sense of serene elegance on this Korean restaurant. Having started with a Purple Tiger (warm saké and Chambord liquor) in the ground floor bar, our dinner continued upstairs with a tasty selection of appetizers (Panchan) and a deliciously fresh steak tartar (Yuk Hwe). For the main dish, do-it-yourself beef rolls grilled in saké (Kal Bi), we followed the directions of our friendly waitress: "Take a lettuce leaf, douse it with some wasabi sauce, add a few marinated onions, chopped garlic, herbs, meat and rice, roll it all together and eat." As much fun as it was tasty. About $35.

BOTTINO / *Italian modernity*
246 10th Ave. & 24th St.
Tel.: (212) 206-6766

Tenth Avenue used to be considered the end of the world, but now *Bottino* is the latest hangout of artists and gallery owners in this up and coming West Chelsea neighborhood. The menu is a renewal of Italian classics like carpaccio and fresh pasta with seafood, and the decor—1950s furniture, a wall of bottles and dark wood—is simple and elegant. If you are a small group, choose one of the tables near the bar with its lively atmosphere or the garden terrace that is covered in the winter, and softly shaded in summer. About $35.

BOUGHALEM / *Romantic American*
14 Bedford St., between Houston & Downing St.
Tel.: (212) 414-4764

If *Boughalem* were in Soho, the line to get in would undoubtedly be unbearably long. Happily, this small romantic restaurant (the type of place that New Yorkers love) chose to set its candlelit, white-clothed tables on a residential street in the West Village—thus eliminating for the moment mandatory reservations and throngs of tourists. The chef James Rafferty has concocted a subtle and inventive "new American cuisine." The cod cakes and roast beet salad with goat cheese are delicious. The waiters are all Frenchies who learned their trade at *Balthazar*: impeccable. About $35.

BRAQUE / *Summer nights*
775 Washington St. & W. 12th St.
Tel.: (212) 255-0709

Only open in the summer, this terrace restaurant adjoining the Industria Photo Studio is a wonderful place to eat out on steamy nights—a lot better in our opinion than *Tortilla Flats*, the well known Mexican place across the street. You can always find a large and comfortable canvas seat at a candlelit marble table. The menu is as satisfying as it is concise. Daily specials—which include seasonal vegetables, grilled fish or fresh pasta—are tasty and the cocktails are generous. When we feel like a good meal, eaten outside and in peace and quiet, we always end up at *Braque*. About $25.

CAFE COLONIAL / *Light lunches*
276 Elizabeth St. & Houston St.
Tel.: (212) 274-0044

At the edge of Nolita, the *Cafe Colonial* gives you an idea why we like Houston Street so much (see inset Outdoors). A rare feeling of space emanates from the outdoor pointillist fresco, the high-beamed ceilings and the bay windows that look onto the Avenue. The Brazilian-accented menu is simple and good, the prices are modest and the cappuccino with its hearty aroma and thick froth is one of the best in the city. About $25.

CAFE GITANE / *Parisian indolence*
242 Mott St., between Houston & Prince St.
Tel.: (212) 334-9552

In a city on the move, this bistro makes you want to kick off your shoes and laze around for hours reading magazines. Unfortunately, it's not so easy, because the *Café Gitane* is always packed. The working class Parisian decor (an old canary-yellow cash register and cooks who wear work shirts from the Peugeot car factory) attracts a hip, young international clientele day and night. The waiters, a bit too business-like for our taste, manage the lack of seating space like rigid accountants, but you can always order coffee and sit on the bench outside, a great spot to be when the sun sets on old St. Patrick's Church across the street. About $20.

CAFE HABANA / *Revamped diner*
17 Prince St. & Elizabeth St.
Tel.: (212) 625-2001

This new restaurant has settled itself in the locale of *Bella's,* an old neighborhood diner, and has kept some of the original fixtures: pale green formica tables and counter, bolted-down bar stools, chrome fans and even some of the good old ridged plastic water jugs. It's also been cleaned up quite a bit to keep in step with today's esthetic kudos. Everything is smooth, clean and strictly no smoking. French fries and onion rings addicts have been replaced by the stylish Nolita crowd who come to nibble grilled corn on the cob while sipping cafe con leche. All that remains of this place's glorious culinary past are the hamburgers and cheeseburgers, still on the menu. About $20.

CAFE ORLIN / *Sunny brunch*
41 St. Mark's Place, between 1st & 2nd Ave.
Tel.: (212) 777-1447

If you're hankering for a real New York breakfast with perfectly golden home fries, softly poached eggs, a crisp salad and a great cappuccino while reading *The New York Times* in the sunshine, *Café Orlin* is your spot. This restaurant's sidewalk terrace is perfect for East-Village people-watching while feasting on one of the best brunches in town. From the Eggs Benedict to the cheesecake, the sandwiches to the soups (try the carrot and coriander), it's all delicious. Open twenty-four hours a day, it's also great when you just want to nosh, meet a date or take a coffee break. About $20.

CHEZ ES SAADA / *Morocco barocco*
41 1st St., between 1st & 2nd Ave.
Tel.: (212) 777-5617

Every single day of the year, the staircase and washrooms of *Chez Es Saada* are sprinkled with fresh rose petals, making for royal entrances into this chic Moroccan restaurant. Ignore the swarm of people at the bar and find yourself a low table in the lounge to sip a pomegranate Martini. Dig into the shrimp with black couscous, a melt-in-the-mouth lamb tagine or a sauteed tilapia (white fish with caramelized onions) while you admire the curvacious belly dancer, all castanets and veils. Straight out of the Arabian Nights. About $40.

DANAL / *Tea-time in the countryside*
90 10th St., between 3rd & 4th Ave.
Tel.: (212) 982-6930

With its hodge-podge antiques, piles of cushions, old patchwork quilts, fireplaces, flowerpots and humming stoves, *Danal* is one of the city's coziest restaurants. It feels like home, safe from the elements and the worries of the world. The English high tea served on Friday and Saturday afternoons (by reservation only) is particularly delicious. For $15, you'll be treated to piping hot tea, cucumber, smoked trout and cream cheese sandwiches, a pile of warm scones dripping with crème fraiche and a large assortment of pastries. About $30 (dinner).

DELICIA / *Viva Brazil!*
322 W. 11th St., between Greenwich & Washington St.
Tel.: (212) 242-2002

We stumbled across this tiny Brazilian restaurant completely by chance. Its street-level windows are non-descript, and the decor inside even more so: white-washed walls, half a dozen tables, a few plants and that's about it. But because we love Brazilian cooking and were sick of the horrendous carioca cantinas on 46th Street, we took a chance and went in—something that we have never regretted! First, the food: *Delicia* offers savory home cooking at great prices. The "bolinho de bacalhau" (cod balls) starter is mouthwatering, mains include perfect "feijoada" (Brazil's national dish—a pork and black bean stew sprinkled with manioc) and a creamy "mucqueca de camarao" (shrimp and vegetable fricassee in coconut milk). The other great thing about this place is the atmosphere: we were drinking our second Capirinha when José, the owner, shoved maracas and tambourines into our hands and invited us to dance the Samba with him for an improvised Carnaval. Three hours later, we were still there, listening to José's old Bahian songs while sipping our "cafezinhou." About $20.

DINER / *Lounge car*
85 Broadway & Berry St., Williamsburg
Tel.: (718) 486-3077
Subway: L to Bedford Ave.

The latest Brooklyn Beauty lies hidden in the shadow of the Williamsburg bridge, surrounded by old, decrepit factory buildings. Encouraged by their experience at *Balthazar* and *Odeon*, the two young owners, Mark Firth and Andrew Tarlow, restored the marvelous patina to this 1927 dining car with a decor of tile mosaics, translucent lamp shades, wooden booths and rounded ceilings. Diner classics like hamburgers, French fries, and T-bone steaks are chalked in daily on a slate along with succulent specials and a list of cocktails to rival the best Manhattan lounges. Simplicity, old-fashioned charm and reasonable prices make *Diner* one of our favorite places. Around $17.

DOWNTOWN CIPRIANI / *Power lunches*
376 W. Broadway & Broome St.
Tel.: (212) 343-0999

The last time we were there, Liv Tyler was eating at the next table. But don't get taken in by the snobbish allure of this classic Soho eatery. *Downtown Cipriani* is one of the best possible addresses for business meetings and other power lunches, not to mention you can always find a table at lunch time. The calm, sunny ground floor dining room is perfect for serious discussions and delicate negotiations. It's also one of the only restaurants in New York that has a "prix fixe" menu served from noon 'til midnight: $28 for an appetizer, main dish, dessert and coffee. In summertime, you can slip up to the rooftop terrace and sip one of the famous Bellini cocktails (champagne and white peach nectar). About $50 (à la carte).

FLORENT / *Night owl haunt*
69 Gansevoort St. & Washington St.
Tel.: (212) 989-5779

A faithful replica of popular 1950s diners, *Florent* is a favorite for Meat Market transvestites, night-club owners, tipsy tourists and other creatures of the night in need of comfort food. At any time of night you can order up a burger & fries, sausage & mashed potatoes or scrambled eggs & bacon. A detail that we loved: the pinch of cinnamon in the coffee—so good that you'll down several refills to the last drop. About $25.

GREAT JONES CAFE / *Cajun hole-in-the-wall*
54 Great Jones St., between Lafayette & Bowery
Tel.: (212) 674-9304

Great Jones is one of the first places our New York friends took us to, and since then, we've become regulars. The specialty of this tiny, smoky, noisy restaurant is southern Soul food served in a very down-home style. The menu is written on the wall, listing boiled shrimp and po'boy sandwiches to be washed down with gallons of Gold margaritas. The food is as honest as the prices, the mood contagious and the juke box famous for its selection of corny old favorites. About $20.

HANGAWI / *Korean vegetarian Zen*
12 E. 32nd St. & 5th Ave.
Tel.: (212) 213-0077

The Empire State Building isn't far off and Fifth Avenue is jammed with people, taxis and tour buses, but at *Hangawi*, you'll hardly notice. Oriental serenity is the hallmark of this vegetarian restaurant, and the wood paneling, low tables and satin seat cushions are worlds away from the street's turmoil. Shoes are discarded at the door, seating is on the floor and talking kept to a whisper—deeply and welcomingly serene. Some of the dishes are a bit bland, and our meat-eating friend Olivier left complaining that he was still hungry. But we loved the tea and beautiful pottery tea set, the green dumplings and the tofu-asparagus salad. About $35.

IL BAGATTO / *Temperamental Italian*
192 E. 2nd St., between Ave. A & B
Tel.: (212) 228-0977

The routine at *Il Bagatto* is always the same. Have you reserved? Of course. Are you on time? Obviously, because if you weren't, your reservation would be down the drain before you could say "Buona Sera." In any case, like everyone else, you'll have to cool your heels for an hour at the downstairs bar before you get your table. And don't even think of complaining, or else it's: Out! So, just order a glass of wine and be patient—it's well worth the wait. The Italian cuisine is fabulous and the prices incredibly cheap—hence the popularity. When you finally do get to your table, you'll savor the scrumptious antipasti, spinach bud or fennel salads, quail with bacon bits and huge plates of fresh pasta. And as a reward for your patience, no one will disturb you if you want to linger after dinner, sipping grappa and smoking a last cigarette. About $25.

LE JARDIN BISTRO / *Home sweet France*
25 Cleveland Place & Spring St.
Tel.: (212) 343-9599

We have a definite weakness for this restaurant, whose garden transports us nostalgically back to the south of France. White-washed walls, soft lights and the thick vines are so a-propos that we lapse into the accent of childhood. The food is lusciously fresh, the wine list remarkable, and the service astonishingly relaxed for a French restaurant. What more could you ask for besides year-round endless summer evenings? About $30.

JUNNO'S / *French-Asian glamour*
64 Downing St. & Varrick St.
Tel.: (212) 627-7995

The milky blue walls, chocolate-colored vinyl booths, long sinuous counter covered in a thick layer of industrial lacquer and a few Japanese Cherry tree branches tell us one thing: *Junno's* decorator must have subscribed to *Wallpaper*. This new restaurant's menu follows the latest trends as well. Fusion cuisine with French, Korean and Japanese accents is served up in artistic compositions on such beautiful plates that you'll wish you could drop a set into your shopping bag (they are the work of Axial, two Soho designers). Keep a bit of space for the ginger crème brulée. If you only want to have a drink, the bar has a long list of exotic cocktails made with saké or Korean vodka. We suggest you come by on late Saturday nights, when *Junno's* sometimes turns into a raging impromptu karaoke scene. About $30.

LUCKY STRIKE / A staple
59 Grand St., between Wooster & W. Broadway
Tel.: (212) 941-0479

What would we do without our Soho hangout, *Lucky Strike?* The success of this bistro—*Balthazar* owner Keith McNally's first—has been constant for the last fifteen years, and it's not surprising. The decor is all cozy wood, mirrors and copper-toned reflections. The service is fast and efficient, everything on the menu is available until 3am, and the food is delicious. Not to mention two other important things, extremely rare for New York: there's always a table available, and smoking is tolerated—just ask for an ashtray. About $25.

MALATESTA TRATTORIA / Neighborly Italian
649 Washington St. & Christopher St.
Tel.: (212) 741-1207

Nothing fancy here! This noisy West Village trattoria built its shining reputation on simple home cooking (we loved the purple artichoke and parmesan salad) and its laidback waiters—so lax sometimes that it borders on hilarious. Some of our American friends find the place chaotic, but we think that it is just quintessentially Latin. Around $20.

MARKT / Beer-mussels-fries
401 14th St. & 9th Ave.
Tel.: (212) 727-3314

The massive oak bar at *Markt* is one of the longest in the city: fifty people can line up here comfortably. So much the better, to serve up the main attraction of this new Belgian restaurant, its fantastic selection of beers—*Stella Arois, Kriek, Leffe, Hoegaarden, Chimay* and other brews rarely available in New York. A replica of the Brussels' *Café de Markt*, with carved wood benches, suspended lights, a huge apothecary with tiny drawers and magnificent painted tiles salvaged from a Flemish church, the result is classic and majestic. The menu is typically Belgian—mussels in white beer, waterzoi and "Salades Liégeoises." $40.

NEXT DOOR NOBU / *The epitome of Japanese food*
105 Hudson St., between Franklin & N. Moore St.
Tel.: (212) 334-4445

Everyone has heard of the Japanese chef Nobu Matsuhisa, but few have been able to get through the door of his famous restaurant. It has been totally booked for more than five years, inaccessible to those who can't make dinner plans four weeks in advance. In order to spread the wealth, Nobu decided to open a simpler place—situated, as the name suggests, one door away. Here, anyone can try to get a seat, because they don't take reservations. You'll still probably have to wait a good hour before getting a table (except maybe on Mondays) but that's the price to pay for sampling this highly acclaimed Japanese cuisine. Nobu's experimentation with texture and the fresh fish really make this place worth the wait. About $50.

ODEON / *Forever chic*
145 W. Broadway & Thomas St.
Tel.: (212) 233-0507

This Tribeca bistro is the exception to the rule that says New Yorkers only go for the newest thing. *Odeon* has been full every night since its 1980 opening, and hasn't lost any of its original lustre. In fact, it's this freshness, coupled with a reliable menu and impeccable service, that makes this restaurant shine. You feel chic, and yet relaxed. No one is there to stalk a celebrity, and even if one were to show up, nobody would care. Patrons are all too busy enjoying juicy T-bones, fries and perfect Cosmopolitans. About $35.

OYSTER BAR / *Long Island Express*
Grand Central Station (underground), 42nd St. & Vanderbilt Ave.
Tel.: (212) 490-6650

To reach the *Oyster Bar*, you first have to walk through the most beautiful railroad station in the world. The main hall of Grand Central Station is a cathedral of steel and stone patronized by more than a million commuters daily. Recently spectacularly restored, the station itself is well worth the visit. The huge domed ceiling has been entirely cleaned, revealing the original aqua-marine color and thousands of tiny luminous stars. Breathtaking. And if you're not catching a train for the seashore, the New England decor of the *Oyster Bar* will make you feel like you're there anyway, with its checkered tablecloths and high, vaulted ceilings. The menu, a large page of single-spaced handwriting chronicling thirty varieties of oysters, superb seafood platters, dozens of the freshest fish, crabs, lobsters and crawfish, is as dizzying as the white wine. Don't forget to taste the creamy New England Clam Chowder. About $45.

OZNOT'S DISH / *Brooklyn's Middle East*
79 Berry St. & N. 9th St., Williamsburg
Tel.: (718) 599-6596
Subway: L to Bedford Ave.

We won't soon forget the dinner we had one fall evening, in this small bohemian restaurant hidden on a residential street in Williamsburg. You'll feel like you're on vacation as you settle into the very West-coast, hippie-chic decor. The wine list is endless. As for the cuisine, the marriage of Afghan, Moroccan and Lebanese flavors is a trip on the Orient Express for the price of a subway token. We suggest that you order as many appetizers as possible and share them. In the summer, the glass ceiling of the rear dining room opens to let you eat under the stars. About $25.

PATOIS / *Cozy bistro*
255 Smith St., between Douglass & Degraw St.
Tel.: (718) 855-1535
Subway: F to Carroll St.

This little bistro is one of the jewels of Carroll Gardens (see Smith Street in the Styles chapter). You have to pass through the kitchen to slip into the marvelous back room that opens onto a garden during the summer. In winter, the crackling stove and smell of wood smoke transform *Patois* into a backwoods log cabin. Alan Harding's menu is as tasty as it is imaginative, mixing Mediterranean tastes and American recipes with a few Indian touches. For example, home made duck paté with grilled figs and pomegranate, curried pumpkin soup, fresh crab and ricotta raviolis, vegetable rolls on mint couscous, and caramel cheesecake with almonds. A word to the wise: Come early because by 8 o'clock all the tables of *Patois* are full, and they don't take reservations. About $30.

PEARL OYSTER BAR / *Ocean flavors*
18 Cornelia St., between W. 4th & Bleecker St.
Tel.: (212) 691-8211

Hardly bigger than a boat cabin, this typical New England restaurant serves simple, fresh and tasty seafood platters. Sit at the counter—there's only one table, anyway—to taste Blue Point oysters, a bucket of steamers or a tasty lobster roll (a fresh bun stuffed with lobster meat), and wash it all down with a glass of dry white wine. The honest tastes and whiffs of fog in this charming bar keep will you coming back for more. About $30.

PLAN'EAT THAILAND / *Thai on the run*
141 N. 7th St., between Bedford Ave. & Berry St., Williamsburg
Tel.: (718) 599-5758
Subway: L to Bedford Ave.

This Thai cafeteria is jammed all day long with Williamsburg residents in search of a quick, cheap and extremely tasty bite. Sit at the counter, where you can spy the six woks sizzling on an ancient stove and marvel at the dexterity of the chef at work. You'll want to taste everything that parades before your eyes: shrimp rolls, coconut milk soups, lemongrass grilled chicken salads, beef with spinach... About $17.

RICE / *Rice of all races*
277 Mott St. between Prince & Spring St.
Tel.: (212) 236-5775

Rice is a great place to stop for a bite when you're on an all-day shopping spree in Nolita. The menu of this small restaurant works on a very clever idea: all kinds of rice (brown, black, Japanese, Italian round, wild, etc.) are available in all sorts of combinations. We loved the spinach rice balls covered in curry sauce, the eggplant sushi and the perfectly caramelized Thai iced coffee. About $17.

ROSA MEXICANO / *Mexican ecstasy*
1063 1st Ave. & 58th St.
Tel.: (212) 753-7407

At *Rosa Mexicano,* everyone starts their meal with a pomegranate margarita and a dish of guacamole—the pulpy pink drink is perfect with the spicy avocado dip freshly prepared at each table. A pure delight. Our appetizers, a sea scallop ceviche and some "taquitos de tinga poblana" (pork tortillas) were sensational. As for the main dish, Lisa the food expert suggested we try the "Cuitlacoche" crepes. Although this dish is the height of refinement for Mexicans, the gooey black parasite mushroom that grows on corn stalks had very strange effects on us: panic, disgust, shivers and—an hour later—the comic relief of uncontrollable laughter. About $40.

RUSSIAN SAMOVAR / *Vodkas, pelmenis and babouchkas*
256 W. 52nd St., between Broadway & 8th Ave.
Tel.: (212) 757-0168

This is where Russian expatriates come when homesickness hits. Mikhail Barychnikov, Joseph Brodsky and Rudolf Noureiev were all regulars. The mischievous owner Roman Kaplan is more than happy to join you at your table for an evening of gossip and strange but true anecdotes about his restaurant. Otherwise sit back and mellow out to the languorous melodies of pianist-singer Alex Zhurbin, sample some of the dozens of flavored vodkas, and if you are hungry, order a dish of smoked fish rather than the more complicated (and less successful) entrées. The *Russian Samovar* is worth visiting, if only to hear the warm Slavic accents and to wonder at the contents of the incredible collection of jars behind the counter. About $35.

SHUN LEE CAFE / *Uptown Chinatown*
43 W. 65th St., between Columbus & Central Park West
Tel.: (212) 769-3888

We crisscrossed Chinatown searching for a worthwhile dim sum place—a palace or a hole in the wall would have done, but with the exception of the exquisite soup dumplings of *Joe's Shanghai* on Pell Street (which is the only good thing in this dreary restaurant), all our attempts were in vain. Giving up the search for authenticity in the Chinese neighborhood, we wound our way uptown to find the *Shun Lee Cafe,* with its tiny shrimp dumplings, fried raviolis with vegetables, juicy roast pork buns and other steaming delights. The waitresses wheel their caddies up to your table and recite the contents in a cloud of vapor. Don't hesitate to lift the metal lids before making your choice. Everything is good, including the four dipping sauces. About $30.

STINGY LULU / *Eccentric diner*
129 St. Mark's Pl. & Ave. A
Tel.: (212) 674-3545

There's always something happening at *Stingy Lulu's*. In the evening, extravagant drag queens do the serving, unless they've decided to show off by breaking into song between the tables. On weekends, neighborhood oddballs wander in for a late afternoon "breakfast." In this strange 1950s diner, everything is available anytime of day and night, the menu is solid, and the decor is priceless: multicolored formica tables, vinyl booths with chrome jukeboxes, kitsch poster ads and paper placemats illustrated with cocktail recipes that you'll want to slip into your pocket. If you run across Karazona, the Kurdish owner, ask him to tell you his story—it's a classic. About $17.

SURYA / *Sophisticated Indian*
302 Bleecker St. & 7th Ave.
Tel.: (212) 807-7770

Surya is one of the darlings of the "Indian chic" trend that is sweeping the city (like *Tabla,* 11 Madison Ave.), in total contrast to the kitsch esthetics of the East Village Indian eateries. Here, everything is smooth, elegant and white: the booths, the long tables and the small lounge area where you can sip a Tajmapolitan (the house drink of vodka, fruit cocktail and cinnamon) while waiting for your table. You're better off ordering an assortment of appetizers, more refined than most of the main courses. Weather permitting, go sit in the garden with its enchanting blue candles and climbing plants. About $35.

TEA & SYMPATHY / *English afternoons*
108 Greenwich Ave. & Jane St.
Tel.: (212) 807-8329

Choose a dreary, overcast day to go get cozy at *Tea & Sympathy*—it will be as if you were snuggled up in the sitting room of an English nanny. A pot of tea and a plate of bangers & mash, Shepherd's Pie or some other standard British fare will surely raise your spirits. The problem: this tiny restaurant is so popular on weekends that the wait outside in the rain or snow can last several hours. But during the week, in off hours, you can linger, sleepily listening to the waitresses' Cockney accents. Before you leave, pop next door to *Carry On Tea & Sympathy*, to pick up thick sausages, shortbread, silly teapots or portraits of the Queen. About $20.

THE GRANGE HALL / *Forties glamour*
50 Commerce St., between Hudson & Bedford St.
Tel.: (212) 924-5246

The Grange Hall is all atmosphere. Hidden in a curve of a winding street—one of the only ones in New York—this warm hideaway boasts impeccable forties elegance. Some will tell you that this is a fantastic dating spot (the bar is crowded with lovebirds from dusk on), but it is also an ideal place to perk up on Sunday mornings with a big brunch and lots of Bloody Marys. About $30.

UNION SQUARE CAFE / *Four stars*
21 E. 16th St. & Union Square
Tel.: (212) 243-4020

This restaurant has been the *Zagat's* (the American bible of eating places) favorite for years, thus making it unavoidable when taking a gastronomic tour. In a classic decor hung with modern paintings, Danny Meyer's team—also the owner of *Grammercy Tavern, Eleven Madison Park* and *Tabla*—serves fantastic American cuisine that varies with the seasons and produce available on Union Square (see Foods chapter). Whether it's tuna tartare, fried squid, roast suckling pig with rosemary, lobster and squash salad or grilled salmon with foie gras, the recipes of this restaurant are miracles for the taste buds, ever renewed and absolutely fresh. The simplest dishes are often the best, like mashed potatoes with garlic and leeks, or even the humble hamburger. About $55.

VONG / *Sensational Franco-Thai*
200 E. 54th St. & 3rd Ave.
Tel.: (212) 486-9592

Exquisite smells will tickle your nostrils as soon as you open the door of *Vong*: a beautiful table in the entry displays the thousand spices used by this Franco-Thai restaurant—one of the first to try "fusion food." The clientele is mostly business, but the gold-leaf-and-wood-screen decor is a refined and exotic experience. Jean-Georges Vongerichten's astounding menu changes daily. The desserts are especially unforgettable: clouds of soft sherbet laced with exotic fruits and trimmed with delicate, crispy cookies, to be savored in that order. About $55.

WILD LILY TEA ROOM / *Tea ceremony*
511 W. 22nd St., between 10th & 11th Ave.
Tel.: (212) 691-2258

Ines Sun, the owner of *Wild Lily*, deserves a big thank you for having opened her tea room so close to all the galleries and you can deliver it after completing the Chelsea tour (see Arts chapter). In this small Zen space, the bubbling sound of the goldfish aquariums mingles with the soft swish of waitresses as they tiptoe by in their slippers. Ceremonially prepared Japanese teas will restore you—*Wild Lily* proposes more than forty varieties of tea, along with small sandwiches, sushi or delicate pastries. On Friday nights, you can also come and listen to violin, flute and other classical concertos. About $25.

YAMA / *Fresh makis*
122 E. 17th St. & Irving Place
Tel.: (212) 475-0969

An ideal spot for a quick lunch, this handkerchief-sized restaurant hides one of the city's best sushi counters. In fact, it looks more like a fish monger's shop than a restaurant, with filets of tuna, salmon and smoked eel piled in cool, wet pyramids. Ignore the menu that is offered, and ask for the list of specials. These makis are rolled and filled before your eyes by silent cooks with surgical precision. About $30.

Arts]

Art is everywhere in New York: in the famous galleries of the Met and the MoMA, of course, but also nestled in the upper floors of downtown industrial buildings, tattooed on the walls and hugging the sidewalks. The Soho district alone counts 190 galleries. But this isn't the only artsy area: art dealers have colonized Chelsea and are beginning to spread to the cold storage rooms of the Meat Market, the wholesale butcher shops that melt into the Hudson river. The distances between these zones is so geographically spread out that someone thought up the Art Shuttle, a free bus that links Chelsea, Soho and the Meat Market. And that's not all. The too-often neglected boroughs harbor all sorts of lesser known treasures such as the Noguchi Museum, P.S.1 Center, or BAM's Majestic Theater. From Long Island City to Chelsea, from Soho to Williamsburg, here are the galleries, record shops, movie houses, experimental theaters and avant-garde institutions where New York's creative energies are thriving.

AMATO OPERA / *Home-made arias*
319 Bowery & 2nd St.
Tel.: (212) 228-8200
www.amato.org

Sally and Tony Amato recently celebrated the triumphant fiftieth anniversary of their opera house. At an age when most people would be thinking about retirement, this astonishing Italian couple continues to produce classical opera in a strange little white building that struggles to stand up on the Bowery. For about twenty dollars, you can listen to Puccini's *La Boheme*, *The Enchanted Flute* or *The Barber of Seville* in a space more reminiscent of someone's living room than the Metropolitan Opera House. The productions are simple, with home-made costumes and flimsy decors, but that's part of the charm. Make no mistake, though, the singers aren't amateurs—most of them are star students of Julliard or the Met itself.

ANGEL ORENSANZ FOUNDATION / *Alternative synagogue*
172 Norfolk St., between Houston & Stanton St.
Tel.: (212) 529-7194
www.orensanz.org

Built in 1850, this old synagogue has been converted into a multi-level performance space and exhibition hall that draws crowds with its slightly decadent opulence and varied program of events. Its owner, the truculent Spanish sculptor Angel Orensanz, hosts a Lou Reed show as easily as an avant-garde photo festival, an Alexander McQueen blow-out, a Maya Angelou reading, a political debate or a Shakespearean play. Whatever happens to be going on at the moment, be sure to check out the magnificent building behind it all.

ANGELIKA FILM CENTER / *Independent filmmaker's mecca*
Corner of Mercer & Houston Sts.
Tel.: (212) 995-2000

True, the screening rooms are miniature, and the aisles that bisect them pretty exasperating (you can never sit facing the exact center of the screen), but the *Angelika Film Center* is one of the rare theaters in New York showing foreign and independent films. This alone is well worth a few inconveniences, don't you think? Coffee in the chandelier-decked foyer with its neoclassic columns and old movie posters is part of the fun.

Chapter 3

BARGEMUSIC / *Water music*
Fulton Ferry Landing on the East River, Brooklyn
Tel.: (718) 624-4061
www.bargemusic.org
Subway: A, C to High St.

Chamber music on the water and a panoramic view of Manhattan's skyline... Seems too good to be true? This Brooklyn barge has made it a reality for the past twenty years. Every Thursday evening and Sunday afternoon, *Bargemusic* offers baroque, classical or romantic recitals ($15-20). June through August, there are additional concerts on Friday evenings as well. After the concert, you can have a drink on the deck, or finish your evening with a cocktail on the terrace of the *River Cafe* just next door.

BROOKLYN ACADEMY OF MUSIC / *Kingdom of the Arts*
30 Lafayette St. & Ashland Pl., Boerum Hill
Tel.: (718) 636-4100
www.bam.org
Subway: 2, 3, 4, 5, D to Atlantic Ave.

The BAM is the cultural pride of Brooklyn, too often disdained by Manhattanites because of its location ("so far") and their insular snobbism. Too bad for them because this music academy, which will soon celebrate its 140th birthday, is one of the most prolific and avant-garde artistic centers in the United States. Throughout the year, dance, music, opera and theater shows fill the roster. In the fall, the fantastic Next Wave Festival invites a plethora of artists from all over. Our favorite last year: the very sober interpretation of an Astor Piazzolla tango-opera by the Gidon Kremer Company put on at the Majestic Theater. Even more beautiful than the main opera house, this recently renovated theater miraculously retains its slightly time-worn decor. The BAM also recently opened the vast Rose Cinema, which specializes in independent and foreign films. One more reason to cross the East River.

CHILDREN MUSEUM OF THE ARTS / Kids' stuff
182 Lafayette St., between Broome & Grand St.
Tel.: (212) 274-0986

Chocolate cake, glue and finger paint are the first things you smell when you enter this museum, dedicated to youngsters from ten months to ten years old. In addition to exhibits by international artists, story-telling hours and different kinds of shows, the museum offers the young artists plenty of workspace. Accompanied by an adult (mandatory—the museum doesn't babysit), kids can make mobiles, puppets, frescoes, or even rehearse their lines in a mini "Actor's Studio."

COSTUME INSTITUTE / Fashion history
Metropolitan Museum of Art
1000 5th Ave. & 82nd St.
Tel.: (212) 570-3908

Hidden in the Met's cellar, the Costume Institute is a fashion museum where you really learn something. Curator and scholar Richard Martin's exhibitions are not only beautiful, but also pedagogical. Two recent ones, dedicated to the invention and evolution of American sportswear (American Ingenuity, 1927-1978) and the Cubist influence on fashion trends (Fashion and Cubism, 1908-1925) once again proved this point. Most of the exhibitions are accompanied by a picture book that can be found in the Museum gift shop. More than simple catalogues, these are definitive reference books for fashion lovers.

DANZIGER / Everything about photography
851 Madison Ave., between 70th & 71st St.
Tel.: (212) 734-5300

The gallery of James Danziger, one of the greatest American experts on photography, mixes every pictorial style—from the nineteenth century to today. In addition to month-long temporary exhibitions, the gallery has maintained an important permanent collection for the past ten years. You can see (and buy) works by Henri Cartier-Bresson, Annie Leibovitz and Sheila Metzner, shots of New York in the 30s by Berenice Abbott, and beautiful portraits of Audrey Hepburn done by Mark Shaw during the shooting of the film classic Sabrina in 1953.

Chapter 3

DEITCH PROJECTS / *Talent scout*
76 Grand St., between Wooster & Greene St.
Tel.: (212) 343-7300

Considered to be the Leo Castelli of the 90s, Jeffrey Deitch built his reputation by discovering young talent, many of whom had only just finished art
school. His gallery is unique. To begin with, contrary to the majority of his
neighbors, his showroom is on the ground floor, permitting you to enter on
a whim, even if just to escape from the urban noise. The exhibitions are
resolutely avant-garde and oriented towards new technology. Some of our
favorite past works: *Bubble World*, a sculpture of luminous globes by R.M.
Fischer, and the incredible TV Tank, by the architectural agency LOT/EK.

DIA CENTER FOR THE ARTS / *Modern Art sanctuary*
548 W. 22nd St. Between 10th & 11th Ave.
Tel.: (212) 989-5566
www.diacenter.org

Inaugurated in 1987, the Dia Foundation is a pioneer, listing Jenny Holzer,
Tracey Moffat and Richard Serra among its finds. Enclosed in white walls
and lit with multicolored neon in the staircase, you can almost reach out
and touch the energy in this place. On the roof, Dan Graham's permanent
installation—one large glass cylinder trapped in another into which you
can wander in and out—recalls the old water towers perched high on the
city's rooftops. On the same busy Chelsea street, you'll also find the
Matthew Marks (243-1650), Morris Healy (243-3753) and Pat Hearn (727-
7366) galleries. And after a busy day touring these, stop in for a well-ear-
ned green tea at *Wild Lily Tea Room* (see Tables chapter).

FAT BEATS / *DJ Heaven*
406 6th Ave., between 8th & 9th St., 2nd Floor
Tel.: (212) 673-3883

Welcome to the vinyl mecca of rap, reggae and R&B. Check out the store's customers, all dressed in the mandatory hip-hop baggy pants, Nikes
and gigantic shirts, and utterly absorbed by the eclectic selection. Brandon,
our friend and favorite DJ, swears by this musical treasure chest and can't
go a week without emptying his wallet at *Fat Beats*, where the stock is
constantly renewed.

FILM FORUM / *Cinema paradiso*
209 W. Houston St., between 6th Ave. and Varrick St.
Tel.: (212) 787-8110
www.filmforum.com

It all began in 1970, with fifty folding chairs, a 16mm projector and a loft on the Upper West Side. Thirty years and three moves later, the *Film Forum* is now comfortably settled in an old print shop on Houston Street and has become one of New York's most respected movie houses. The recipe for success? A subtle combination of U.S. and foreign independent films, retrospectives and old classics. After numerous complaints, the direction has finally decided to sell—you guessed it—popcorn. Don't feel guilty indulging, as it earns $100,000 per year for this non-profit organization.

FOOTLIGHT RECORDS / *Singin' in the rain*
113 E. 12th St., between 3rd and 4th Ave.
Tel.: (212) 533-1572
www.footlight.com

When the crooner Tony Bennett was searching for one of his early out-of-print recordings, he found it at *Footlight Records*. In CD and vinyl, this record shop possesses the entire soundtrack of mythical America: musicals, Broadway hits, big band, lounge music, cabaret shows and vocalists. The employees know the tunes by heart and can reel off their stock at the snap of a finger.

GAGOSIAN GALLERY / *High circles*
980 Madison Ave., between 76th & 77th St.
Tel.: (212) 744-2313

To enter Larry Gagosian's sumptuous duplex gallery, you have to cross an intimidating lobby under the inquisitive eye of the doorman and then take a private, wood-paneled elevator to the top. This Upper East Side gallery of mythical reputation represents, among others, Andy Warhol, David Salle, Yves Klein and Richard Serra. The nec plus ultra of chic and expensive contemporary art, an endless hallway leading on to spotless, vast rooms with subtle lighting lets the art speak for itself. Also check out *Gagosian Downtown* (136 Wooster St., 228-2828).

Chapter 3

GALLAGHER PAPER COLLECTIBLES / *Precious archives*
120 E. 12th St., between 3rd & 4th Ave.
Tel.: (212) 473-2404
www.vintagemagazines.com

Located in an East Village basement, this incredible shop is one of the best-kept secrets in town. Descending a rusty metal staircase, you proceed past the furnaces, push open a heavy door and tiptoe through a long, narrow corridor that finally leads to the heart of this shop which is blanketed in monastic silence. Newspapers, magazine, and rare archives are piled in a huge labyrinth. *Playboys* from the 1950s, outdated Italian magazines, issues of *House Beautiful* dated 1912, *Vogue, Vanity Fair* and *Harper's Bazaar* from 1910 to today, old sailing periodicals—the list goes on. Lots of incognito stylists and designers haunt this place, looking for inspiration in yesterday's fashions. Michael Gallagher and Mary Browne, the owners, have also recently opened a small gallery/bookshop in Chelsea that specializes in fashion. In addition to the beautiful photo exhibits, you can find all of Gallagher's old magazines here, as well as a rich selection of books on fashion and design that can be bought or consulted on site. Browne Gallagher Gallery, 601 W. 26th St., 14th floor, tel.: (212) 924-9208.

INTERNATIONAL CENTER OF PHOTOGRAPHY /
Photography from all angles
1130 5th Ave. & 94th St. **Tel.: (212) 860-1777**
1133 6th Ave. & 43rd St. **Tel.: (212) 768-4682**

Both a school and a museum, ICP is probably one of the most beautiful homages to the art of photography ever created. Founded in 1974 by Cornell Capa (Robert's brother) and at first dedicated to photo-journalism, this institution currently explores every incarnation of the instant image, from single-frame artistic exposures to holography, fashion photography, digital images and video. Man Ray, David Seymour, Weegee, Bruce Davidson and Marc Riboud are only a few of the thousands of names that ICP has exhibited over the years. We suggest that you first visit the Midtown Center, whose seamless architecture and modern programs are stunning. For those who would like to sharpen their eyes and improve their technical prowess, workshops are organized every weekend at the Uptown Center (around $300 per workshop).

ISAMU NOGUCHI MUSEUM / *Sculptures and stones*
32-37 Vernon Blvd., Long Island City, Queens
Tel.: (718) 204-7088
www.noguchi.org
Subway: N to Broadway, Queens
Open from April to October

Isamu Noguchi, who died in 1988, became famous for the delicate lamps he designed after WWII to breathe new life into the Japanese paper lantern industry. But above all, this man was a genius in sculpture. The old brick warehouse on the East River that displays his work is an invitation to touch and feel. But you'll have to resist the urge to slide your fingers on these monolithic sculptures with textured filigrees and masterful contrasts of smooth and rough, because "fingertips contain soils that leave a dirty residue, causing damage." On the other hand, you can have a drink in the small cafe, sitting in one of Charles Eames' famous Eiffel Tower chairs. The rock garden, with its fountain and exotic trees in tortured poses, is a marvelous composition of calm and serenity.

KIM'S VIDEO & MUSIC / *Big films for small screens*
6 St. Mark's Pl., between 2nd & 3rd Ave. **Tel.: (212) 505-0311**
350 Bleecker St. & 10th St. **Tel.: (212) 675-8996**
www.kimsvideo.com

There are several *Kim's Video* shops in New York, and each branch has its own identity. The common point: a large selection of videos, for sale or for rent, that can't be found anywhere else. At Kim's West, on Bleecker St., more than 8000 cassettes are organized by general themes (classic, black & white, foreign films, cult movies, science fiction, contemporary, etc.) and then classified by director. The employees are all young independent film fans, and present daily specials of their choice, often some hilarious unknown, or that long-forgotten film classic you've been meaning to catch. This is the place for film fans tired of Hollywood excess.

LEO CASTELLI / *The patriarch*
420 West Broadway, between Prince & Spring St.
Tel.: (212) 431-5160

Beware: You are entering mythical territory! For the past fifty years, the man who discovered Jasper Johns, Roy Lichtenstein and Andy Warhol has inspired both museum curators and buyers with his sharp eye for contemporary art. Leo Castelli died last summer at age 91, but his namesake gallery is keeping the spirit alive. The gallery and its rich archives—open to writers, editors and historians—might be moving uptown soon, so stay tuned for the new address.

MEAT MARKET DISTRICT / *Meaty art*
Between 14th St. & Horatio St., 8th Ave. & West Side Drive

After Soho and Chelsea, the Meat Market is the new "in" place for art. The galleries are rushing to set up business between the slaughterhouses and cold rooms of this old New York neighborhood. On 14th Street, between 9th and 10th Avenues, you'll find the vast *Heller Gallery*, the *Long Fine Art,* the *Rare* and the *Tate Gallery,* which is managed by a former assistant of the influential Mary Boone. Among our favorites: *Trans Hudson Gallery,* one of the area's pioneers, at 416 W. 13th Street. Young talents from the world over are exhibited here by Joseph Szoecs. *White Columns,* an association of New York artists, has opened at the corner of Horatio and W. 4th Street and presents impressive exhibitions of innovative work.

MOMENTA / *Culture shock*
72 Berry St., between N. 9th & 10th St., Williamsburg
Tel.: (718) 218-8058
Subway: L to Bedford Ave.

Momenta opened its doors in Williamsburg about four years ago when several New York artists, fleeing the stratospheric Manhattan rent hikes, converged in this Brooklyn neighborhood. Today, Momenta is the local cultural center, whose mission is to help discover local talent who haven't yet been spotted by the major Manhattan dealers. Most of the work exhibited is being shown for the first time, which turns this gallery into a showcase for emerging currents, notably computer installations and video images. While you're in the neighborhood, you should also check out Pierogi 2000 at 177 N. 9th Street (718-599-2144) and Roebling Hall, S. 4th and Kent Ave., both innovative and intriguing spots.

MUSEUM AT F.I.T. / *Fashion for everyone*
Corner of 7th Ave. & 27th St.
Tel.: (212) 217-5800
www.fitnyc.suny.edu

The Fashion Institute of Technology's museum is entirely dedicated to fashion—fashion history, materials and fabrics, and the major concepts of the industry. This should come as no surprise, as this place has produced some of the biggest names in American fashion. Visitors will discover the works of Isabel and Ruben Toledo (see Styles chapter), revisit Claire McCardell's "American look," learn about the Asian influence on current trends, and even glimpse tomorrow's big names. This is an absolute must for fashion students, and a gratuitous pleasure for everybody else.

MUSEUM OF TELEVISION & RADIO / *Transmission territory*
25 W. 52nd St., between 5th & 6th Ave.
Tel.: (212) 621-6800
www.mtr.com

On a freezing January afternoon, we spent several exquisite hours here watching old episodes of the *Twilight Zone*. Whether you want to see the complete *Star Trek* series or a specific episode of *Bewitched*, listen to Woody Allen's radio interviews or to Martin Luther King in Washington, consult early commercials, or shiver while listening to *The War of the Worlds*, this boob tube paradise offers more than 75,000 programs that can be watched on small individual screens. There are also three projection rooms with soft, deep armchairs facing a wide screen that change their programs daily. Admission: $6.

NEW YORK EARTH ROOM / *Get grounded*
141 Wooster St., between Houston & Prince St.
Tel.: (212) 473-8072
Open from September to June

The *New York Earth Room* is a living, breathing work of art. Even before you see it, your nose, which has long since become accustomed to exhaust fumes, will experience something new: the smell of forest undergrowth. At the end of a long corridor, an immense, somber, silent installation rises before your eyes: artist Walter de Maria dumped 197 cubic meters of earth in this big white loft, 1300 tons that have been bravely supported for the past twenty years by the metallic structure of this old

Soho print shop. If the smell of the soil is still so fresh, it's because the curator, Bill Dilworth, takes great care of it. Each week, he waters, hoes, and turns it over—and occasionally harvests a mushroom or two.

NEW YORK PUBLIC LIBRARY / *History and technology*
5th Ave. & 42nd St.
Tel.: (212) 930-0800

Two stone lions guard the front and the trees in Bryant Park shelter the back. The *New York Public Library* has always been a peaceful haven for readers, researchers and urban dreamers. Since its recent $15-million renovation, this venerable institution has also become as high-tech as any Silicon Valley company. Thanks to forty-eight work stations and thirty additional tables equipped with electricity, you can plug in your laptop and work away in the soft light of the old copper lamps. Every American daily newspaper and magazine (as well as some foreign publications) can be consulted in the periodicals room on the first floor.

OTHER MUSIC / *Alternative records*
15 E. 4th St., between Broadway & Lafayette St.
Tel.: (212) 477-8150
www.othermusic.com

How can such a tiny record shop survive, living in the shadow of the giant *Tower Records* right across the street? It's easy. As its name suggests, *Other Music* sells everything that its big neighbor doesn't: Japanese imports, kitschy compilations of cocktail music, experimental jazz, French pop from the 1960s (Brigitte Bardot or Francoise Hardy), and, of course, a very diverse collection of electronic music. In fact, *Tower's* employees often send clients with hard-to-satisfy, overly specific requests to shop here.

PHUN PHACTORY / *Graffiti museum*
45-14 Davis St., Long Island City
Tel.: (718) 482-7486
www.phunphactory.org
Subway: E, F to 23rd St, 7 to 45th Rd.

Sitting flush under the overhead subway rails, a few steps away from P.S.1, an out-of-use Queens factory stands out from its grim surroundings by a burst of explosive colors. The *Phun Phactory* is unique: it is the first outdoor gallery devoted to spray paint. Pat DiLillo, the founder, launched his idea in 1993 to promote graffiti art by obtaining legal spots "to allow artists to channel their talents in a constructive—rather than destructive—way." With broken windows, a caved-in roof and a choreography of breathtaking mural frescoes, the result is one of the most surprising buildings we've ever seen. The artists are only allowed to paint after having submitted photographs of past productions, and the works are renewed about every three months. Brushes, obviously, are forbidden—here, it's spray paint only.

P.S.1 / Revolutionary museum
22-25 Jackson Ave., Long Island City, Queens
Tel.: (718) 784-2084
www.ps1.org
Subway: E, F to 23rd St., 7 to 45th Rd.

An old public school converted into a center for contemporary art in the 70s, P.S.1 re-opened in 1997 after yet another majestic renovation. This museum's exhibits are experimental and innovative, accentuating the genius of works by Gordon Matta-Clarke, Ronald Bladen, Sol Lewitt and Alfredo Jaar. Not to be missed: the awesome installation *Meeting* by James Turrell that can only be visited at dusk (light plays an integral part in this work). During the summer, P.S.1 is the theatre for an astonishing musical festival. In a half-happening, half-rave atmosphere, strange installations such as a giant refrigerator, a touch-and-feel tower, and a tent inflated with helium serve as a backdrop for several international DJs that groove with a tight crowd of hip city dwellers—pretty original for a respected cultural institute! P.S.1 is serene, awe-inspiring, and continually pushing the definitions and limitations of art.

PEARL PAINT / Artist emporium
308 Canal St. & Greene St.
Tel.: (212) 431-7932
www.pearlpaint.com

If you have any artistic flair, *Pearl Paint* will be your nirvana. This temple of art supplies, a mainstay of Chinatown for the past sixty years, has an immeasurable inventory of art supplies. All you have to know is that an entire floor is dedicated to paint brushes, another to watercolors, oils and acrylics, and the third floor is for paper and canvas. The diversity of tools and materials for sale seems infinite, and the prices couldn't be better. New Yorkers know it too, and the staircases of this building are constantly crowded with young artists from the East Village as well as better known painters from Tribeca looking for a rare color or a special grain of paper.

SCREENING ROOM / *Brunch at Tiffany's*
54 Varick St. & Canal St.
Tel.: (212) 334-2100
www.thescreeningroom.com

In a wind-beaten industrial wasteland two steps from the Holland Tunnel, the *Screening Room* is the ideal place to wind up a New York weekend. Hide behind big sunglasses, have a taxi drop you off at the corner of Canal and Varick around noon and order brunch at the restaurant. With its red neon LIQUOR sign, the ceiling fans straight out of *Casablanca,* and the round, luminous Art Deco globes, you can imagine you've won the leading role in a 1940s movie. After eating, hurry next door to grab a seat in the movie theater in time for the weekly, ritual projection of Blake Edward's masterpiece, *Breakfast at Tiffany's.* Every Sunday at 1:15pm.

ST. JOHN THE DIVINE / *Angelic meetings*
1047 Amsterdam Ave. & 112th St.
Tel.: (212) 662-2133

This sublime Gothic cathedral can seat 3000, not counting the innumerable angels perched in the upper reaches. Of course, there are church services here, but Baroque concerts, children's shows and philosophical seminars are also part and parcel of the program at St. John's. Set aside an hour when all is quiet in the church, kneel down silently on one of the prayer benches, and you'll hear the flapping of wings among the ceilings vaults. Angels? Perhaps. Or maybe a young peacock who's escaped from the courtyard. A tiny, secret rose garden is also hidden in the back, but we'll let you find that on your own.

STALEY-WISE / *Glamour world*
560 Broadway & Prince St.
Tel.: (212) 966-6223
www.staley-wise.com

At a time when fashion photography was judged too pretty to be a real art form, Etheleen Staley and Taki Wise opened the first gallery in Soho exclusively dedicated to fashion and Hollywood glamour. Since then, staged frivolity has earned recognition in its own right. Collectors now want vintage prints by Frank Horvat, Lee Miller, Man Ray and Helmut Newton. Much of this is due to the persistent efforts of this groundbreaking gallery that has been exhibiting the best fashion photographers of the world for the past twenty years. Each exhibition enriches the permanent archives, which are open to the public.

THE KITCHEN / *Avant Garde noshers*
512 W. 19th St., between 10th & 11th Ave.
Tel.: (212) 255-5793
www.thekitchen.org

The Kitchen has been open for twenty-five years, serving up crop after crop of avant-garde New York artists. Phillip Glass, Laurie Anderson, Bill T. Jones, Brian Eno, Peter Greenaway and Bill Viola all made their debuts here. The center welcomes every form of expression, be it video, musical, dance, film or literary, as long as it is innovative and subversive. The latest offering that ties neatly in to the center's origins is TV Dinners, where video artists talk with the public and explain their works—all while nibbling on a gourmet buffet.

THREAD WAXING SPACE / *Eclectic gallery*
476 Broadway, between Broome & Grand St.
Tel.: (212) 966-9520

The eclectic programs offered by this non-profit organization set it apart from other galleries. You might just as easily stumble across an exhibition of terrifying nineteenth-century medical instruments on loan from the Philadelphia Museum as a comparison study of Beck's art and that of his grandfather, Hal Hansen, or a homage to Archigram, the visionary utopian group of 60s British architects. Aside from five annual exhibits which include painting, photography, and sculpture, the gallery also hosts contemporary dance and religious music shows, opera, multimedia events and theater.

VISIONAIRE GALLERY / *Enlightened art*
11 Mercer St. & Canal St.
Tel.: (212) 274-8959
www.visionaireworld.com

On a desolate street at the edge of Soho, this brand new gallery is the first permanent incarnation of the magazine *Visionaire*, a prestigious publication printed in limited editions with the most extravagant backing. Devoted to the art of fashion, the gallery has already showcased the works of painter-illustrator Ruben Toledo, creations by Viktor & Rolf and a retrospective on the magazine itself.

ZIEGFELD THEATER / *Theatrical cinema*
141 W. 54th St., between 6th & 7th Ave.
Tel.: (212) 765-7600

One needs a good Hollywood blockbuster every now and then and the Ziegfeld Theater is the best place for it. Despite its recent conversion into a multiplex, this historic former home of the Ziegfeld Follies retains its baroque decor. The screens are enormous and the acoustics incredible. Films like *Titanic*, *X-Files* or *Star Wars* always premiere at the *Ziegfeld,* and this is where we come with our cine-maniac friends when they try to persuade us—despite our violent protests—that something like *Jurassic Park* is a quality film.

ART FESTIVALS

ANCHORAGE FESTIVAL (info: 206.6674 ext 252; www.creativetime.org)
May-June

This very underground music and performance festival is held inside one of the foundations of the Brooklyn Bridge (Brooklyn side, Cadman Plaza West). The line-up in this gigantic gothic-industrial complex includes acoustic improvisations, battle of the DJs and experimental shows. Information and tickets at Other Music (see text).

MIDSUMMER NIGHT SWING (info: 875.5766; www.lincolncenter.org/swing)
June-July

Five times a week for two months, the Lincoln Center organizes an open air marathon ball. Rumba, salsa, or tango, couples make it and break it around the Fountain Plaza (63rd St. & Broadway). Lessons at 6:30 pm, dancing from 8 pm ($11 an evening).

BRYANT PARK SUMMER FILM FESTIVAL (info: 512-5700; listings *Time Out*)
June-August

Just after sundown every Monday evening in summer, this tiny park behind the Public Library (6th Ave. & 42nd St.) is the meeting place of movie buffs. Classic films like *Forbidden Planet, Vertigo, The Wizard of Oz,* and *The Big Sleep* are shown for free, projected on a giant screen smack in the middle of the skyscrapers. Come early with something to eat, a sweater, and a blanket to spread on the grass.

SHAKESPEARE IN THE PARK (info: 539-8750; www.publictheater.org)
June-August

This has been a New York tradition since the early 60s: every summer, anyone can go and enjoy Shakespeare at the outdoor Delacorte Theater in Central Park (at the 79th St. entrance). *Hamlet, Titus Andronicus, The Tempest* and many other of the great playwright's masterpieces have been produced here. Pick up your tickets in the park at the Delacorte, or at the Joseph Papp Public Theater (425 Lafayette St.) and keep an eye out for the free performances—usually one show per year.

SUMMERSTAGE (info: 360-2777; www.summerstage.org)
Mid-June-mid-August

Music fans of all persuasions throng to Central Park (Rumsey Playfield, near the 72nd St. entrance) for this fantastic outdoor festival showcasing musicians from the world over. The entrance is free, beer flows, people dance between the chairs, and when it gets too hot to breathe, the organizers shower the crowds with ice water. Sultry daytime World Music concerts are followed by cool evening performances by the New York Grand Opera. Magical.

DOWNTOWN ARTS FESTIVAL (info: 243-5050; www.simonsays.org)
September
This huge pluridisciplinary and experimental festival (music, theater, dance, contemporary art, happenings, new media) stretches from Chelsea to the East Village by way of Soho. Hundreds of artists participate every year. For your convenience: the free Art Shuttle takes you from one neighborhood to another. (info bus: 769-8100; www.artshuttle.org)

NEW YORK FILM FESTIVAL (info: 875-5050; www.filmlinc.com)
September-October
Unlike its European cousin in Cannes, the New York Film Festival is accessible to common mortals. All you have to do is buy your tickets—in advance—at the Alice Tully Hall, Broadway & 65th St. The selection covers a wide range of independent and international films, including World Premieres.

ART UNDER THE BRIDGE (info: (718) 624-3772)
Mid-October
With its post-industrial atmosphere of old warehouses converted into artist studios, the Dumbo neighborhood (Down Under the Manhattan Bridge Overpass) is one of Brooklyn's most intriguing areas. During this festival organized by the Dumbo Art Center, you can visit studios, watch "conceptual parades," happenings on the banks of the East River and party in empty factories.

NEXT WAVE AT B.A.M. (info: (718) 636-4100)
October-December
This is one of the most exciting avant-garde programs in the city, including modern dance performances, concerts and other brilliant and creative never-before-seen spectacles. (See text on Brooklyn Academy of Music.)

Chapter 3

READINGS

WRITING NEW YORK
Edited by Phillip Lopate, 1998: a massive anthology that dresses a rich literary portrait of New York through the texts of Charles Dickens, Edgar Allan Poe, Vladimir Maiakovski, Celine, Allen Ginsberg and a hundred other authors, from the beginning of the century to the present.

GOTHAM HANDBOOK
by Sophie Calle and Paul Auster, 1997: a strange little New York how-to by the American author and the French artist who experimented with passers-by and a public telephone booth.

LOW LIFE
by Luc Sante, 1991: a voyage into the belly of New York at the turn of the century. Corruption, alcoholism, brothels, gambling joints and dens of iniquity—everything that made New York famous and infamous.

NEW YORK
by Paul Morand, 1929: proof that, although the city is in permanent flux, it hasn't really changed that much.

MANHATTAN TRANSFER
by John Dos Passos, 1925: this fundamental, fresco-like novel is a patchwork of New York stories and characters ranging from a millionaire stock broker to a starving immigrant to a fame-hungry Broadway actress.

Our New York Press Review:

TIME OUT NEW YORK
For its "Clubs" section and its "Pick of the Day" column.

NEW YORK MAGAZINE
For its food critics and its "Gotham Style" pages.

PAPER MAGAZINE
To take the pulse of the latest New York trends.

NEW YORKER
For its inventory of exhibitions and its literary chronicles.

VILLAGE VOICE (free)
For the fashion column by Lynn Yaeger.

NEW YORK PRESS (free)
For its wacky astrology section, "Sign Language" by Caeriel.

Styles]

New York, fashion capital of the world? In the early nineties, the very idea made Europeans snicker, convinced, as Paul Poiret put it in 1922, that "American designers don't have the spark of genius and American women are always three years behind the times." Today, nobody would dare snub American designers. Luxury-goods mogul Bernard Arnault recruits young talent in Manhattan, offering them management positions in established French couture houses. The Austrian Helmut Lang settled in Soho to "understand the times." With an unquenchable thirst for trends and fads, New York compulsively invents and consumes new styles. No one needs a guide to get around the miracle mile on Madison Avenue, so the places we've chosen are mostly downtown, where fashion is constantly conquering new territory: after Nolita, designers are now setting up shop next door to the wholesalers and old drugstores on the Lower East Side. And because style is a passion that isn't only a question of clothing, this chapter also includes the best places for furniture and interior design.

A DETACHER / *Mona's world*
262 Mott St., between Houston & Prince St.
Tel.: (212) 625-3380

Mona Kowalska likes to design clothes and travel around the world. Her gallery-boutique in Nolita is a reflection of just those passions: a personal ready-to-wear line (long skirts in padded nylon, blouson jackets, printed silk shirts), mixed with a few select items that were found either in the U.S. or abroad. Photography books, jewelry made in Ecuador, Bettye Muller shoes, Spanish water glasses, antique linen sheets and beautiful vases by Nigel Coates are artistically arranged on a long, low shelf.

ALPHAVILLE / *Retro toys*
266 West Houston St., between 6th Ave. & Varick St.
Tel.: (212) 675-6850
www.alphaville.com

Although *Alphaville* is a toy shop, most of the clients are nostalgic adults revisiting their childhood. Steve Garchin and Kary Graut, the owners, sell mint-condition vintage toys and pop-culture collectibles: old metal robots, psychedelic spinning tops, Star Trek figures, crackling cap guns, rulers with holograms, games and miniature space ships. From Wonder Woman to Spider Man to James Bond, all the mythical heroes are here, as well as B-movie posters and tacky old advertising signs.

AMY DOWNS HATS / *Heads up!*
103 Stanton St. & Ludlow St.
Tel.: (212) 598-4189

Nestled in Amy Downs' tiny canary-yellow shop, the hats seem to be having a party of their own. In felt or wool, trimmed with feathers, veils or beads, these flirtatious and charming hand-made head-dresses are each more seductive than the last. It makes us miss the times when hats were a mandatory fashion accessory. Prices: between $50 and $120.

ANNA SUI / *Gothic queen*
113 Greene St., between Prince and Spring St.
Tel.: (212) 941-8406

In the gray minimalist world of NY fashion, Anna Sui's creations are definitely out of place. But provocative night creatures, rock stars and femmes fatales partial to dramatic silhouettes have nonetheless remained faithful. Like her style, the decor in Sui's boutique is both funny and macabre. Violet walls, weirdly shaped armchairs and mannequin heads make for something of a cross between a saloon and the Addams Family's mansion. Morticia would adore these crochet dresses, fringed leather jackets and gothic laces as much as she'd go for the wickedly sophisticated new cosmetic line.

ANNEX FLEA MARKET / *Second-hand treasures*
6th Ave., between 25th & 27th St.
Tel.: (212) 243-5343
Every weekend

If you're a sucker for second-hand furniture, vintage frocks and Americana, you'll love this place. Just to give you an idea, here are a few of the things we found on our last expedition: a red-iron chair and rocking chair for $30, a mint-condition 1940s camera, a designer aluminum garbage can, four Martini glasses and a beautiful patchwork quilt. We left the market glowing, certain that we'd picked up the deals of the decade. You should know, though, that the market's dealers do their buying in Connecticut and on the northern banks of the Hudson—if you have the time and the inclination, you can find the same goods there for a fraction the price.

ANTIQUE BOUTIQUE / *Vintage and rock & roll*
712 Broadway, between 4th St. & Astor Place
Tel.: (212) 460-8830

The only antique thing left in this shop is its name. For a long time, it specialized in American second-hand clothes for men and women, but it recently gave itself a new look in order to house the complex and audacious creations of Stephen Sprouse, Jeremy Scott, Kitty Boots and the Englishman Joe Casely-Hayford. Nevertheless, there is still a vintage department, where you can find a fabulous collection of 1960s polyester men's shirts, and all sorts of lurex sweaters and fur coats for the ladies. At the very least, take a peek at the always-intriguing window displays.

APC / *Radical normality*
131 Mercer St., between Prince & Spring St.
Tel.: (212) 966-9685
www.apc.com

Jean Touitou, the designer behind *APC,* launched his label in 1988 with a small mail-order catalogue. More than ten years later, he can brag that his is the only young French design house operating on an international scale. His recipe for success? Using the best of what France has to offer—craftsmanship of traditional manufacturers—to make everyday clothing with impeccable proportions in excellent textiles. His unwashed denim blue jeans, woven on old-fashioned looms, created a new, worldwide standard: an almost cardboard-like stiffness with 1950s finishings and long, long legs that have to be rolled up. Everyone copied it. In addition to his ready-to-wear, Touitou has begun to offer lifestyle items that emphasize pure and simple products: Tunisian olive oil, motorcycle helmets and perfumed candles.

CATHERINE / *A French woman*
468 Broome St. & Greene St.
Tel.: (212) 925-6765

The guiding light and owner of this namesake boutique is Catherine Malandrino, who also happens to be head designer for Diane von Furstenberg. A tribute to French femininity, her new Soho boutique is as tangy as a violet bonbon. Mauve handbags, cruise dresses straight from a James Bond film, lavender felt cowboy hats, hot-pink high heels by Michel Perry (designed exclusively for Catherine), Weiss candies and Brigitte Bardot's silly little songs in the background all make for a suave and cosmopolitan mix.

CLUB MONACO / *Carbon copies*
160 5th Ave. & 21st St. (one address among many)
Tel.: (212) 352-0936
www.clubmonaco.com

We weren't going to mention chain stores in these pages, but we had to make an exception for *Club Monaco.* This Canadian chain is a must for anyone who wants the New York look at podunk prices. The current trends are copied with such wit and efficiency that you leave the shop feeling you've just bought out Marc Jacobs, Michael Kors and Helmut Lang. Of course, the fabrics are less luxurious, but everything else is there: pleated skirts just under the knee, twin sets with three-quarter sleeves, and the tiny flannel handbags that were on every catwalk.

COMME DES GARCONS / Monumental couture
520 W. 22nd St., between 10th & 11th Ave.
Tel.: (212) 604-9200

There has never been a shop so deserving of its art gallery neighbors: the new temple of the avant-garde designer Rei Kawakubo is a masterpiece of architectural futurism. Prepare yourself for a shock while crossing through the cylindrical metal tunnel that serves as an entrance. Inside the store, the space is broken up by massive panels of curved walls, so that you can never see all the clothing at once. You have to stroll between these barriers to discover a pair of shoes here, a few dresses there and a handful of accessories further down the passage. The dressing room is hidden behind a thick, black curved wall that resembles a Richard Serra sculpture. The back wall, in polystyrene, is strictly off-limits, under the threat of immediate expulsion from the museum, oh, excuse me—the store.

CROCODILE / Country things
17 Bleecker St., between Mott & Elizabeth St.
Tel.: (212) 473-8465

"I always wanted to get a job that let me drive a big truck." By opening *Crocodile,* Gwen found a solution to her problem. Every month, this delicate twenty-seven-year-old blond leaves to criss-cross southern Virginia and Kentucky looking for American antiques from the 20s and 30s: fans, shakers, mirrors, lamps and pottery in creamy colors of ivory, almond green and grayish blue. Gwen also has a thing for childhood reminiscing: wall maps, school desks and one-of-a-kind toys.

DDC LAB / Hip eclecticism
180 Orchard St., between Houston & Stanton St.
Tel.: (212) 375-1647

This recent addition to the heart of the Lower East Side participated in the hastened gentrification of the neighborhood. Good or bad? Not for us to judge. The latest creations of owners Roberto Crivello and Savania Davies-Keller are the mainstay of this ultra-hip boutique, where you can also find the moment's most chic (and most expensive) accessories: Jackie Chan Pump

Fury Reeboks ($300 to $2,500 a pair), Spoon watches from Japan and Naomi Goodsir cowboy hats. You can drink a cappuccino at any hour at the in-house coffee bar, and leaf through a large selection of international magazines. Some Sunday evenings, the young owners also organize champagne parties.

DUH / Little bags
102 Suffolk St., between Rivington & Delancey St.
Tel.: (212) 253-1158

Her handbags are all the rage in New York accessory shops. Today, the young Etsuko Kizawa sells her collection in her own boutique, a handkerchief-sized space nestled at the bottom of the Lower East Side. In solid-color fabric or embroidered, garnished with a moiré ribbon or a mother-of-pearl button, slim envelopes or puffy triangles, her creations are chic and practical—and reasonably priced (between $40 and $80). While you're there, make a detour to *Patch 155* on Rivington Street east of Suffolk, a new boutique that showcases several upcoming designers.

FORM AND FUNCTION / Retro modern
95 Vandam St., between Hudson & Greenwich St.
Tel.: (212) 414-1800

New Yorkers' cult-like fascination with post-war design has found its temple. *Form and Function*, located in a huge West Soho warehouse, is an ode to the skeletal structures, pure lines and molded plastics of the 1950s masters. "The generation that grew up with this furniture is now able to buy back its childhood memories," states the owner, Jack Feldman, in an effort to explain the rush for creations by the Eames or Californians Grata Graussman and Milo Baughman. His selection also includes a series of Heifetz lamps praised by the MoMA, and an entire wall of multicolored transistors, globe-shaped televisions and record-players dating from the 40s to the 70s.

FROCK / "A very stylish girl"
225 E. 5th St., between 2nd & 3rd Ave.
Tel.: (212) 533-1013

If Holly Golightly lived in the Manhattan of the 90s, she'd probably shop for her little felt dresses, curved jackets, short trousers and poplin shirts in this East Village boudoir. The two designers, Jenna Na and Erin Pedisich cut and stitch in the back room, creating perfectly proportioned, classically feminine clothing in soft, delicate fabrics.

GANSEVOORT GALLERY / *Chic American furniture*
72 Gansevoort St. & Washington St.
Tel.: (212) 633-0555
www.gansevoortgallery.com

Behind its impressive iron awning of high-tech gears, the *Gansevoort Gallery* hordes a treasure of rare and superb 1930s-to-1960s American pieces: chrome lamps, ebony coffee tables, chiseled ceramics, Eames, Noguchi and Frank Lloyd Wright furniture. This gallery-shop also organizes annual exhibits like, recently, the Modern Nordic Movement, an exceptional collection of objects in glass, ceramic, wood and silver from Scandinavia.

GEOFFREY BEENE / *The master*
783 5th Ave., between 59th & 60th St.
Tel.: (212) 935-0470

The young designers of the Fashion Institute of Technology swear by him, and his dresses are regularly exhibited at the Met. Geoffrey Beene was one of the first designers to free himself of the Parisian fashion dictates and create the foundations for what would become American style—a style that sublimates the silhouette without ever hampering the body's movements. At seventy-two, the inventor of chic sportswear is still hard at work. He continues to experiment in this tiny, laboratory-boutique on Fifth Avenue, where the decor is as solemn as a couture house (note the pretty wall of silhouettes drawn by Joe Eula). You can order made-to-measure dresses or pick through a fun and interesting ready-to-wear line.

HELMUT LANG / *The world according to Helmut*
80 Greene St., between Spring & Broome St.
Tel.: (212) 925-7214
www.helmutlang.com

In 1997, Helmut Lang packed up lock, stock and barrel and headed for Manhattan, leaving the European fashion world in a state of shock. This austere majestic space designed by Richard Gluckman is now the only place in the world where you can glimpse his complete collections, displayed in a maze of black and white walls. The dressing rooms, almost as big and just as bare as the rest of the store, have only one colorful touch: a LED sculpture by artist Jenny Holzer that spells out troubling aphorisms. Those who think, like we do, that the prices have skyrocketed beyond reason, should visit the store as a museum, if only to pay homage to this master of minimalism.

HOTEL OF THE RISING STAR / *Conceptual ready-to-wear*
13 Prince St. & Elizabeth St.
Tel.: (212) 625-9659

"We're a company interested in the development of a language with regard to product culture and the space between potential and reality." Excuse me? The trio of architects and designers that hide in this Nolita boutique's backroom take fashion very seriously. Their label reads "Organization for returning fashion interest." So, to pique our interest, these three young fashion fans offer a selection of "political" books and design a ready-to-wear collection that is both unisex and anti-trend—big basic pieces, camouflage prints on raw canvas, straight shirts—that remind us strongly of Jean Touitou's work at *APC*. And what else? They also rent out post office boxes, and you must admit that "The Hotel of the Rising Star" makes for a pretty great mailing address.

ISABEL TOLEDO—THE LAB / *Creative Yin & Yang*
277 5th Ave., between 29th & 30th St., 5th floor
Tel.: (212) 685-0948

Isabel and Ruben Toledo never do anything like anyone else. Sculptural, fluid, draped and geometric, Isabel's clothing designs stand out from all other New York fashion. This designer's boutique is located in the rug merchant's neighborhood. You have to ring a bell to get in, then take an elevator to the fifth floor. When you arrive, it's the designer herself who welcomes you, unless it's her bubbly hubby offering you a cup of fresh Cuban coffee. Spread throughout the vast space, his breathtaking paintings and sculptures evoke Dali, Magritte and Goya. You will be treated more like an old fiend than a potential client, which is a breath of fresh air in the murky fashion world. Yes, you guessed it: we adore this couple, and we want the whole world to discover their talents, their generosity and their incredible originality.

JIMMY CHOO/ *Choose Choo's shoes*
645 5th Ave., on 51st St. between 5th & Madison Ave.
Tel.: (212) 593-0800

According to many, Jimmy Choo is Manolo Blahnik's heir apparent. By installing himself recently in this luxurious boutique, the shoemaker that so delighted Lady Diana proves that he's definitely the competition. His creations are as delicate and precious as those of the Grand Master of feminine footwear—candy colored cruise sandals, diamond-studded high heels, tiny satin or mink mules—but the prices are less expensive ($300 to $1,000).

LANGUAGE / *Fashion alphabet*
238 Mulberry St., between Prince & Spring St.
Tel.: (212) 431-5566

In this eclectic boutique, located in an old Nolita ceramics factory, painter Ana Abdul and her husband Lipe Medeiros propose an entire lifestyle that includes fashion, furnishings, art and beauty. Helter-skelter, you will find pashmina shawls, Chinese medical cabinets, fresh scented candles, Colette Malouf hair accessories, hand-made Mexican bead necklaces, copies of *Visionaire* magazine, cocktail dresses by Jerome l'Huillier and an interesting selection of American and Brazilian designers (Robert Funk, Tufi Duek, Rosa Cha). The shop also sells Lipe Medeiros' furniture, couches and armchairs assembled with pieces of scaffolding.

LE CORSET / *Chic lingerie*
80 Thompson St., between Broome & Spring St.
Tel.: (212) 334-4936

It's a well-known fact: finding pretty lingerie in the U.S. is almost impossible. This Soho mini-boutique will appease those women who are tired of the synthetic undies made by *Victoria's Secret.* Le Corset offers a colorful selection of antique pieces (Victorian nightgowns, 40s-era slips and real antique silk stockings), as well as lingerie by young American designers like Ellen Berkenbilt and Leigh Bantivoglio that are worn by the top models who live nearby.

LITTLE O / *Vintage for kids*
1 Bleecker St. & Bowery
Tel.: (212) 673-0858

After hunting through flea markets and used-clothes dealers in Oregon looking for clothes for her son, ex-model Debbie Dieterling realized that she wasn't the only one looking for an alternative to Gap Kids. So she opened *Little O*. Ever since, New York's stylish young parents have been streaming to *Little O* to buy Atari jackets in silver vinyl, Petit Bateau undershirts from the 70s and 80s, tiny Pierre Cardin sweaters, old Osh Kosh overalls, and organdy baby dresses à la Shirley Temple. There is also a large selection of logo T-shirts, including Pacman, Superman and Adidas.

LUCIEN PELLAT-FINET / *The prince of cashmere*
226 Elizabeth St. & Prince St.
Tel.: (212) 343-7033

At a time when cashmere was still synonymous with plaid scarves and golden-age fashion, Lucien Pellat-Finet was the first designer to use this material to dress the contemporary silhouette. That was in 1992. He sold his snug-fitting sweaters in quadruple threads from his Parisian apartment and satisfied customers made his reputation. In spite of the recent deluge of cashmere in American fashion, the Pellat-Finet creations are always recognizable for their perky details (stripes, lurex threads, Mondrian-like color patterns, zippers and hoods), their body-hugging cut and... their exorbitant prices.

MANOLO BLAHNIK / *Legendary stilettos*
31 W. 54th St., between 5th & 6th Ave.
Tel.: (212) 582-3007

The high priest of stilettos has moved to a new luxury space, entirely covered in white wall-to-wall carpeting, but his followers from the four corners of the world didn't take long to find him. Fashion victims, foot fetishists and everyone who is elegant in New York fight over his delicate high heels, ultra-fine boots, leather tap shoes and embroidered mules without even glancing at the astronomical price tags.

Chapter 4

MARC JACOBS / *Street couture*
163 Mercer St., between Houston & Prince St.
Tel.: (212) 343-1490
www.marcjacobs.com

An old garage with bare walls, mahogany flooring and a few white leather couches designed by Christian Liaigre—this is where New York's darling of fashion design has chosen to show his creations. The same luxurious minimalism characterizes his clothes. Jacobs is known for having transformed with a wave of his wand the basics of American sportswear (jogging suits, hooded jackets) into beautifully cut must-haves in opulent fabrics. The prices of his cashmere sweaters, shirts with gathered sleeves and "school girl" pleated skirts are even more intimidating than the salespeople's attitudes, but when sale time rolls around, the discounts can reach 70%.

MAYLE / *Lolita style*
252 Elizabeth St., between Hudson & Prince St.
Tel.: (212) 625-0406

The creations of the sexiest couple in Nolita, ex-model Jane Mayle and her companion Chris Travis, are both delicate and wearable. Formerly called *Phare*, their tiny shop, in pastel colors, white tiles and filled with the soft scent of jasmine is packed with cardigan and v-neck cashmere sweaters, fluid trousers and vaporous flowered blouses. The menswear line, designed by Travis, features great shirts and perfectly tailored suits. A few antique camisoles, embroidered handbags and travel souvenirs are also scattered here and there in the shop, adding to its already romantic elegance.

MOSS / *Industrial design*
146 Greene St., between Houston & Prince St.
Tel.: (212) 226-2190

When this boutique first opened its doors in 1995, the world's architectural and design press devoted many pages to describing its "revolutionary concept." A "select shop" before they ever existed, it offered a cutting edge choice of products displayed in the windows like museum pieces. The owner, Murray Moss, knows better than anyone how to tell which way the winds of fashion are blowing, and how to make the most of everyday objects: bouquets of light bulbs by the Dutch Droog, magazine racks and CD shelving in perforated metal by Blu Dot or mural frescoes of the Colab collective—a modern and innovative collection.

MXYPLYZYK / *Useful and useless trinkets*
123-125 Greenwich Ave. & 13th St.
Tel.: (212) 989-4300

Mixi-pli-zic. That's how to pronounce the wacky name of this little shop. All in shades of silver, beige, black and ivory, it's full to the brim with chic knick knacks: stainless steel coat hangers, lamps on articulated stands, steel mirror frames, the latest in travel bags and suitcases, and a plethora of hip gadgets in brushed aluminum. The perfect place to find an elegant, last minute gift.

PEARL RIVER MART / *Chinese bazaar*
277 Canal St. & Broadway
Tel.: (212) 431-4770

Located at one of Chinatown's busiest intersections, *Pearl River* is a miraculous grab-bag of essentials. We always shop there for satin slippers, instant shrimp soups, embroidered silk change purses, paper lanterns, gold-flecked writing paper, green teas and rose-scented dusting powder. You can also find the tai-chi slippers worn by all the models in the Helmut Lang shows (ten pairs to a package).

RESURRECTION / *Second-hand couture*
217 Mott St. between Prince & Spring St.
Tel.: (212) 625-1374

Pierre Cardin's incredible "satellite" coat, a circular rain cape in red and white vinyl from 1969, is displayed in the window next to a long, multi-colored redingote by English designer Ossie Clark. With its sharp selection of 60s and 70s American and European designers (Pucci, Courreges, Saint-Laurent, Halston, Rudi Gernreich and Stephen Borrows among others), this is a mecca for those who love rare vintage clothing. John Galliano, Anna Sui and Martine Sitbon are all regulars, shopping for themselves and using it as a source of inspiration. New Yorkers throw themselves on the futurist garments of Cardin and Courreges, lingerie and cashmere twin-sets from the 50s. This boudoir-boutique also has great accessories like sunglasses, scarves, hats and handbags (mostly Gucci and Hermes). The shoe collection is among the largest we've seen, but you'll have more luck if you have tiny feet.

SHANGHAI TANG / *Modern Orient*
667 Madison Ave., & 61st St.
Tel.: (212) 888-0111

"Re-Orient Yourself." David Tang, emperor of the Hong Kong fashion world, conquered Madison Avenue with this slogan. Displayed on three floors, his accessories, homeware linens and luxurious clothing have modernized the Chinese fashion-passion of the 30s and 40s. Embroidered Mao jackets, silk pajamas, brightly colored "cheongsams" (traditional dresses) and slippers are available for men, women and children. On the second floor, "imperial tailors" are available for made-to-measure clothing.

SHI / *Poetic design*
233 Elizabeth St. & Prince St.
Tel.: (212) 334-4330

Thanks to this small Nolita boutique, the poetic creations of the French Tsé & Tsé Associates are finally available in New York. This is where you'll find the wonderful cubist garland (an electric light garland with cubes of Japanese oiled paper), the lazy vase (a teardrop-shaped piece of glass, suspended by a metal wire) and igloo candleholders that made the two French designers famous. Shi also proposes a disparate selection of antiques, ranging from old Chinese furniture to Gitane ashtrays and Ricard water jugs from French cafés, along with an assortment of mugs, bowls and Asian tea cups. The ceramic crackle vases of Joe Conforti, in white or colored, are among our favorites.

SIGERSON MORRISON / *Star slippers*
242 Mott St., between Houston & Prince St.
Tel.: (212) 219-3893

This store is dangerous—each time we go, we're nearly run over by a client leaving under a sky-high pile of shoe boxes. Kari Sigerson and Miranda Morrison's creations seem to have been designed for the feet of Brigitte Bardot, Monica Vitti or Audrey Hepburn—and induce fits of serial buying. With supple, shiny leather, perfect arches and pale green leather linings, they are both feminine and wearable, sophisticated but never over-the-top.

SMITH STREET / *Shopping in Brooklyn*
Metro: F to Carroll St.

For a shopping spree outside Manhattan, this pretty Carroll Gardens street is ideal. It is filled with young designers' shops and second-hand dealers and the prices will make you wonder why you didn't come sooner. Begin with **Frida's Closet** (#296, tel.: (718) 855-0311) with ready-to-wear inspired by Frida Kahlo. A few doors down, **Astroturf** (#290, tel.: (718) 522-6182) specializes in 1950s: cocktail sets, mixers, toasters, ashtrays, ice crushers, record players, etc. Next, stop at **Stacia** (#267, tel.: (718) 237-0078), a little girl's dream boutique. The young designer sews delicious dresses in tulle and sequined voile on the premises and displays a selection of tiny handbags and beauty products. Last stop: **Hoyt & Boyd** (#248, tel.: (718) 488-8283), a kids clothing store offering, among other things, colorful bonnets and tiny mittens in angora. Let yourself fall completely in love with this neighborhood by finishing the day with dinner at *Patois* across the street (see Tables chapter).

SPRING STREET MARKET / *Bargain basics*
Corner of Spring St. & Wooster St.

From a distance this small, outdoor clothing market may look a bit ordinary. But this is where we go to shop for our basics: straight fluid skirts, lycra tank tops, fitted sweaters and nylon pedal pushers. The quality is basic but the prices are low and the cut, fabrics and colors are always up to date. Made by little known New York designers (Lord of the Fleas, Jeal & Lior, Body Basics, etc.), these clothes are twice the price in trendy shops in the Village.

STEVEN ALAN / *Downtown hip*
60 Wooster St., between Spring and Broome St.
Tel.: (212) 334-6354
www.stevenalan.com

New York owes Steven Alan the return of Clarks as well as the current rush for G-shock watches. His profession? Cool Hunter (aka: fashion forecaster). In his Soho boutique, he has gathered up the best creative clothing and accessories that New York has to offer. Along with the collections of Rebecca Danenberg, Pixie Yates, Daryl K., Cake and Built by Wendy, he showcases sneakers and high-tech handbags, and a plethora of watches by Zucca, Casio and Katherine Hammett. Also check out the *Steven Alan Outlet* in the East

Village (330 East 11th St. between 1st & 2nd Ave.), where the same items are at half the price, taken from the other shop to make room for new arrivals.

SWAY / *Fluid asymmetrics*
84 E. 7th St., between 1st & 2nd Ave.
Tel.: (212) 505-0490

The first time we went to *Sway*, we were looking for pants, but happily we found much more: a long peach-skin dress, a flared stretch skirt, an organdy petticoat and a beautiful blouse in crimson cotton. Spaniard Elena Bajo's designs are natural and sophisticated, fluid and ethereal. Her discreet asymmetries are truly inspired and her fabrics are surprisingly supple and modern. A small menswear collection offers classic cuts spiced up by a sober or playful detail: a pleat, a hole, a visible seam or a stripe of color.

TOTEM / *Modern fetishes*
71 Franklin St., between Church & Broadway
Tel.: (212) 925 5506
www.totemdesign.com

Despite New York's recent craze for 1950s design, a few diehards still believe there is life after Charles Eames. Gail Schultz and David Shearer belong to this group. Their boutique *TOTEM* (an acronym for The Ojects That Evoke Meaning) is on a mission to promote the best of contemporary design. Included are Karim Rashid's nestled tables, rugs by Tom Dixon, James Irvine couches, sponge lamps by Anton Angeli, lacquered screens by David Khouri and small furniture by Ross Menuez: forty designers are represented in all. Every month, the shop launches one designer's exclusive line, complete with an opening night cocktail party that has become a highlight of city nightlife.

VIVIENNE TAM / *Experimental Chinoiseries*
99 Greene St., between Prince & Spring St.
Tel.: (212) 966 2398

Mao-red walls and majestic panels of sculpted wood provide the backdrop for Vivienne Tam's Asian-inspired collections. But make no mistake: this New York china doll's creations offer much more than meets the eye. Traditional Chinese details (dragons and officer collars) are only pretexts for all sorts of futurist experimentations, and the result is much closer to Jean-Paul

Gaultier than Imperial style. Her semi-transparent tattoo dresses and spider-web tunics are all the rage among hip young New Yorkers.

ZERO / *Trendy recipe*
225 Mott St., between Prince & Spring St.
Tel.: (212) 925-3849

First, take hip fashion photographer Mark Borthwick whose fans include the readers of *Face, ID* and *Vogue*. Next, exhibit his pictures alongside the signature line of clothing featuring high-tech fabrics and asymmetric cuts made by his wife Maria Cornejo, a former stylist at *Joseph*. Add a pinch of minimalist furniture by Fernlund and Logan and mix in a few avant-garde creations by the German team Bless. Blend it all together and you get *Zero*, one of the freshest places in town. The clothing is made on the premises, so new styles in limited quantities appear almost daily.

THE RETRO RAGE

"THE WALLPAPER GENERATION"—
this is how *The New York Times* christened the generation of thirty-somethings who tossed out their IKEA furniture to embrace post-war modernism. Now only boomerang tables, molded plastic chairs and futurist lamps will do. These pieces come from a time when a few visionary designers grabbed on to the latest technological advancements like fiberglass to produce furniture on an industrial scale. From Soho to Lafayette Street, dozens of boutiques (*Modernica, Depression Modern, 280 Modern*) specialize in the furniture of Swedish designers like Arne Jacobson, Alvaar Alto and American national heroes Charles and Ray Eames. This same esthetic has also crept into the nightlife scene: the hippest lounges (*Moomba, Veruka, Joe's Pub*, etc.) are all decorated in mid-century modernism. The bar *Lot 61* is furnished with 1950s couches taken from a psychiatric hospital, and the restaurant *Bottino* has more than a hundred vintage Charles Eames chairs. Clothing hasn't been neglected either: in the flea markets and at auctions, New Yorkers fight over vinyl rain capes, astronaut jumpsuits and futurist mini-skirts by Pierre Cardin, Paco Rabanne and Courreges, all circa 1968. "This esthetic is seductive because it reflects a radiant optimism, an immense, blind faith in the future," explains Jack Feldman, owner of the shop *Form and Function*. "We need this kind of optimism to face the next century, not an IKEA couch."

BEAUTY

Beauty]

A new social phenomenon has hit New York like a tornado: beauty. In Soho, cosmetic boutiques have taken over from the art galleries. Uptown, clinical hair factories are opening up one after another. Throughout the city, the number of day spas has increased tenfold over the last three years, but it can still take months to get an appointment in some of them. New York women swear by aromatherapy and natural products. They collect essential oils, stock cucumber masks in their refrigerators, wrap themselves in freshly grated ginger, reserve powdered-almond rubdowns, and moisturize with whole milk. From the corner drugstore to the high-class day spa, here are the places that will surprise, invigorate, and relax you during your stay.

5S / *New age products*
98 Prince St., between Mercer & Greene St.
Tel.: (212) 925-7880
www.five-s.com

5S is the name—acronym for five senses—that Shiseido chose for its second line, less expensive but just as irresistible as the first. The boutique is a curious cross between a new-age pharmaceutical laboratory and a little girl's dream, with mingle tables that invite clients to try products and share beauty secrets. Charm, the pale mauve and slightly iridescent body dusting powder, is sensational. You will also find small accessories imported from Japan, like eyelash curlers and the astounding oil-absorbing paper that keeps your face in perfect balance.

ANGEL FEET / *A walk in the clouds*
77 Perry St. between Bleecker & W. 4th St.
Tel.: (212) 924-3576
www.angelfeet.com

On a pretty paved street in the West Village, *Angel Feet* is heaven in a shoebox. Two armchairs hidden behind a screen, a brick wall and a few plants are the only decoration in this beauty center that dedicates itself exclusively to your feet. "What we do here is not massage, it's reflexology," insists Barbara Morrison, the owner. With classical music in the background, Rachel and Barbara fondle your tootsies from ankle to toe, touching on every one of the foot's 140 nerve endings. The experience can be slightly painful, but after a half-hour massage ($40; $70 for an hour) you'll walk out of the shop on air. In a city where walking is the best mode of transportation, *Angel Feet* is an absolute must.

ASTOR PLACE HAIRSTYLISTS / *Express cuts*
2 Astor Place & Broadway
Tel.: (212) 475-9854

Gentlemen, don't be put off by the odd assortment of unmatched chairs, crooked mirrors and fading photos that decorate this busy beehive hair factory in Noho. And, don't be dismayed by the more than one hundred hairdressers that work on three floors. Even if our friend Mike made us promise not to tell, you only need to remember one name: Nat. He works downstairs in the basement, handles the electric razor like a 50s pro—and for $11 and in less than ten minutes, he'll give you a perfect haircut. You can walk in at any time of day without an appointment. Just grab a ticket and wait your turn.

Chapter 5

AWAY SPA / *Exotic cures*
Hotel W, 541 Lexington Ave. & 49th St.
Tel.: (212) 407-2970

On the fourth floor of the new W hotel masterminded by David Rockwell, *Away* is a part-Californian, part-Asian oasis on the East coast. The decor is pure and simple, all bouquets of wheat and basalt rocks. The beauty care sessions range from the standard manicures, massages and facials to the unusual. A color therapy session ($50) begins by photographing your aura (the end result is a sort of fluorescent Polaroid) followed by a colored effervescent bath, the color depending on which shakras need re-adjusting. For those who prefer something more down to earth, the "Javanese Lulur" ($150) is the pre-nuptial beauty treatment of Javanese princesses: a massage is followed by a rice, turmeric, sandalwood and jasmine exfoliation, a floral bath, and finally, an all-over yogurt wrap. *Away* offers weekend packages that include one or two nights at the hotel ($600 - $800).

BIGELOW PHARMACY / *Beauty grab-bag*
416 6th Ave. & 9th St.
Tel.: (212) 533-2700

"If you don't find it anywhere else, try *Bigelow's*." This is the slogan of the apothecary shop founded 160 years ago and still going strong. The pride of Greenwich Village residents, this old New York pharmacy-drug store-herbal medicine shop stocks an astounding selection of products. Fern soap and tortoise-shell barrettes, shaving brushes and baby bottles, essential oils and homeopathic remedies, rust-proof tweezers and boar-bristle hairbrushes, botanical shampoos by Phillip B. and Potter's cough drops. You'll find everything here, from the most old-fashioned brands to world-renowned labels. One of a kind, *Bigelow's* will have you making daily trips to stock your medicine chest.

BLISS / *Hip spa*
568 Broadway & Prince St., 2nd Floor
Tel.: (212) 219-8970
www.blissworld.com

It's a well-known fact: you have to wait at least a year before getting an appointment with Marcia Kilgore, the founder and star facialist of *Bliss*. But it is less known that it takes only three weeks for a massage appointment and a few days for a pedicure. Hidden in an alcove, the pedicure chairs are velvet thrones. The prices are high, but who could resist a beauty treatment for tired feet in lukewarm almond milk, followed by a sea salt exfoliation? ($52 for an hour; $35 for a regular pedicure.) If you really want to test *Bliss'* star recipes (oxygen facial, "Ginger Rub" or "Lower Body Blaster" for cellulite), explain to the receptionists that you are only in New York for a few days; they may have a last-minute cancellation. *Bliss* also sells a selective range of products, like the amazing Remede creams, aromatherapy lipsticks by Tony & Tina and Diamancel nail files—and for these, no appointment necessary, you can fill up your beauty case any time, or order by Internet or telephone at 888-243-8825.

CHELSEA BARBERS / *Traditional barbershop*
465 W. 23rd St., between 9th & 10th Ave.
Tel.: (212) 741-2254

Real old-fashioned barbers are a dying breed. This is a great reason to sing the praises of Betty Garcia's little venture which offers shaves and haircuts ($15 each) the way they used to be—with shaving cream and brush, scissors and flat razors. There are only two seats, and they don't take appointments, so you might have to wait up to an hour. Don't complain though—this gives you the time to read the paper inside and out. Brandon tested the place for us: "It's the best haircut I've had in years!" he declared on the way out.

ELIZA PETRESCU / *High brows*
Avon Center, 725 5th Ave. & 57th St.
Tel.: (212) 755-2866
www.avon.com

Eliza Petrescu became a star in a few months: people cross Manhattan for a visit, and she is booked solidly for the next five months despite the $60 price tag. What is the specialty of this esthetician who practices on the upper floors of the Avon Institute? Eyebrows! Only in New York could someone become famous for her tweezers. This Romanian immigrant who claims to have been obsessed by eyebrows since the age of nine works miracles with her brushes, scissors and pencils. "Eyebrows are a determining factor in a face's balance," she says. "By redesigning them, you can change an expression, make a chubby face seem thinner, and soften a severe one. It's a question of proportions." By the time she finishes her sentence, she's given you an angelic new face, à la Gene Tierney.

ENFLEURAGE / *Inebriating scents*
321 Blecker St., between Christopher & Grove St.
Tel.: (212) 691-1610
www.aromata.com

A wonderful little store hides behind this unusual name (which describes a way of extracting floral essences). Open the door and the bewitching aromas may have you buying out the store. Not such a bad thing here—it's impossible to go wrong. *Enfleurage* offers the purest essential oils on the market, hair perfumes from Africa, resins to burn over coal, biological soaps and even delicious "Aromatherapy of Rome" candles (actually made in Texas). We broke down and bought the neroli night cream from the house line and some fresh beauty masks sold by the ounce and concocted daily by the owner, Trygvé Harris. Her mixtures of clay, natural essences, oats, lentils and rose buds are highly experimental and work wonders on your skin.

ERBE / *Poetic waxing*
196 Prince St., between McDougal & Sullivan St.
Tel.: (212) 966-1445

What do you look at when you're getting waxed? The ceiling, usually, and *Erbe*'s is a dream, filled with blue and white clouds. If you add to this an operatic aria and the soothing aroma of essential oils, you'll never want to leave this plush ivy-covered beauty salon. Aromatherapy fans will love the house's beauty products that were inspired by old Italian herbalist recipes. Kate Moss and Naomi Campbell have them delivered by the pound.

FRESH / *Fragrance bar*
1061 Madison Ave. between 80th & 81st St.
Tel.: (212) 396-0344

Launched eight years ago by two Russian immigrants who settled in Boston, *Fresh* cosmetics have become the darling of New York glossy magazines that swear by the brand's luxurious milk soaps, peony lotions and honey lipsticks. In the back of the shop, in an immaculate luminous space, visitors can play at the perfume bar, trying on fragrances like orange/chocolate, lavender/coriander or pure bergamote. Other internationally-renowned lines like l'Erbolario, Côté Bastide and Esteban are also available.

GAD COHEN / *Hairdresser to the stars*
313 W. 22nd St. between 8th & 9th Ave.
Tel.: (212) 366-0302

When he isn't off on a film shoot, or lurking behind stage at a fashion show, Gad Cohen works at home in a boudoir that he converted into a workshop. A couch, swivel chair, big mirror, shelves crammed with hairbrushes and scissors, and loads of shampoos and gels from *Kiehl's* make up the decor of this improvised salon. Gad will welcome you with a glass of wine and invite you into his living room to inspect your hair and offer suggestions. His aim, contrary to most renowned hairdressers, isn't to sign his name in your tresses but simply to make you "as beautiful as possible." He'll wash your head upside down in his kitchen sink and give your hair the time it needs—all afternoon if necessary. This stylist only sees four or five clients a day (Isabella Rossellini and Ashley Judd, among others). And his prices are in proportion to his talent: from $100 to $300 for color, $250 for a cut.

KIEHL'S / Legendary products
109 3rd Ave., between 13th & 14th St.
Tel.: (212) 677-3171

Even if *Kiehl's* products are available almost everywhere now, nothing should stop you from visiting this incredible pharmacy where they've been sold since 1851 when a Russian emigrant fresh from his studies in herbal preparations at Columbia University decided to set up shop. With its well-worn linoleum, metal showcases, haphazard lighting and faded photographs of war planes, *Kiehl's* remains a typical East Village bazaar-boutique, a change from Soho's sanitized beauty shops. The salespeople, all dressed in white nurse jackets, are friendly and generous with their advice and samples. As for the products (with names so clinical they become lyrical), they're so good that nothing more need be said. From the incredible Lip Balm #1 to the yellow Silk Groom conditioning cream, to the Unusually Rich But Not Greasy At All Hand Cream with sunscreen, everything at *Kiehl's* is a necessity.

OSAKA / Shiatsu massage
37 W. 46th St., between 5th & 6th Ave. **Tel.: (212) 575-1303**
50 W. 56th St., between 5th & 6th Ave. **Tel.: (212) 682-1778**

In the heart of midtown, this Oriental therapy center is a strange, closed universe where a spartan Japanese serenity eclipses the frenzy of New York. Forget your old habits, ignore your apprehensions, and let yourself be guided (in very halting English) by Mr. and Mrs. Kim. You'll be wrapped in a towel and sent into the steam baths, followed by a cold shower. Next is the sauna and then a grotto-like room with moss-covered walls where you will alternate three times between hot and cold baths—for "rejuvenation" they say. Finally you will be laid upon a table in a dark little room, and a slender masseuse dressed like a Judo instructor will rub your joints, muscles and nerve endings—first with her hands, and then, by standing on your back with her feet. Take a deep breath: the strength and precision of these heels and toes are stupefying; closer to a Sumo wrestling match than a massage. Two hours and $100 later, you'll leave invigorated—with a clear head and restored body—an effect that can last up to five days. Careful: dainty bodies and scaredy cats should abstain.

RED SALON / Intimate beauty parlor
323 W. 11th St., between Greenwich & Washington St. **Tel.: (212) 924-1444**
203 W. 20th St., between 7th & 8th Ave. **Tel.: (212) 645-1114**

Far from the austere minimalism of uptown hair factories, Red Salon is a refuge in the West Village. Intimate, human and personal, this salon has only three chairs, separated from each other by red velvet curtains. Brad Langtry and his assistants will do everything in their power to make your visit a pleasant one. After a skull rub with essential oils, you will be delicately shampooed, and to top it off, you'll get a hand massage while the nurturing creams act on your head. At this point, let Brad take over—he knows what is best for your hair. A hair dressing treasure: cuts from $45 to $85, color from $90.

RESCUE / Aromatic treats
21 Cleveland Pl. & Spring St.
Tel.: (212) 431-3805

Recently opened in Nolita, this brightly colored little boutique with cool marble floors offers aromatherapy-enhanced manicures, pedicures and waxing. Your feet will soak in water perfumed with essences of rosemary, lemon or ylang-ylang before being massaged with scented and invigorating oils. The wax used to remove unwanted hairs contains honey, tea tree and chamomile essences, known for their softening virtues. Rescue also sells a precious range of products: we particularly recommend the Baume de Rose and the exhilarating lotions of Essential Aromatics.

SOHO NAILS / Cheap manicures
458 W. Broadway, between Houston & Prince St., 3rd floor
Tel.: (212) 941-5970

This salon, in a scarcely decorated Soho loft, hasn't raised its prices since the day it opened in 1989: $6 for a manicure, $15 for a pedicure and a mere $18 for both. There's no slick decoration, and no elegant products line the shelves here, only great professionals who know how to wield a nail file and apply polish so that your nails will stay impeccable for a week. Uptown ladies make the trip to Soho just to have their nails done here, and the clientele includes a lot of men as well, who settle for a light buff.

SUITE 303 AT THE CHELSEA HOTEL / Mythical style
222 W. 23rd St., between 7th & 8th Ave.
Tel.: (212) 633-1011

This is one of Manhattan's best-kept beauty secrets. Aside from the sober #303 painted in black, there is nothing on the door. However, three of the city's most talented hairdressers have set up shop in the *Chelsea Hotel*, where international rock stars used to party in the 70s. Armando Corral, April Barton and Marie Delucie, tired of the huge, impersonal Madison Avenue salons, decided to create a bohemian place where artists, models and musicians would feel at home. You'll find a robe in the bathroom and coffee fixings in the kitchen. The salon itself is a large room with yellow walls and aluminum chairs, and looks out onto a flowered balcony. Don't be intimidated. Despite the VIP look of the clientele, nobody here will look down at you. A creative and personalized haircut costs about $70.

WARREN TRICOMI SALON / *Baroque institute*
16 W. 57th St. & 5th Ave., 4th floor
Tel.: (212) 262-8899

Perched on the fourth floor of a nondescript building, *Warren Tricomi* is a baroque temple devoted to beauty. In a joyful disorder of clutter and light, the decor is a cross between a Moroccan bazaar and a Venetian palazzo. From the velvet poufs and Persian rugs, to the copper pails, purple drapes, cast-iron tables and golden gauze draped across the entrance to the pedicure room, everything here is a study in opulence. Other than a cut, style or color by maestro Joel Warren, you can have your nails done by Roxanna Pintilie, be made up or get a henna tattoo, or have Vanessa, the psychic consultant (on Wednesdays) do your Tarot. Perhaps you'd prefer to sit at the tea bar and nibble a cucumber sandwich. Whatever your fancy, don't miss the ladies room: the blown glass sinks and lamp shades look like something out of Arabian nights.

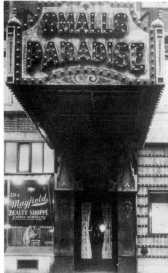

Chapter 5

TRENDY PRODUCTS

FOR FOREIGNERS ONLY

Anyone heading to New York from abroad knows that, despite globalization, there are some things that you can only find in the United States. Most of these products can be bought cheaply in any neighborhood drugstore (*Bigelow's*, for example): epsom salts to invigorate tired feet, the Tweezerman's incredible tweezers, the Great Lash Mascara by Maybeline used by professional make-up artists, Lubriderm body cream, Supersmile whitening toothpaste or the tiny pots of Carmex that keep lips soft. For beauty care, the Remede line (the exfoliator Sweep and the moisturizer Alchemy, in particular) Kiehl's, 5S and Fresh get all the votes. But it is the profusion of hair products that is most dazzling: Countless products to unfrizz, shine, nourish, fortify, soften or moisturize are available everywhere. The Aveda line and the Frizz-ease products by John Frieda are considered to be some of the best. The first aid kit by Bumble & Bumble is now available for the public, originally invented to save the overly styled hair of models during Fashion Week. On the accessory front, New Yorkers love the bra straps head bands (Bumble & Bumble again) and the hairpins, barrettes, bobby pins and nets by Colette Malouf, sold with little picture books (Chignon twist, French twist and Stick twist) that teach you how to do your own hair.

FOODS, ETC.

Foods, etc.]

Whether you're out for a stroll and some tongue-teasers, for a quick snack or to whet your appetite for a special dinner party or to fill a crate of New York delicacies to ship back home, here is a list of the best places to experience the tastes, smells and colors of New York. From locally grown produce to exotic imports, check out the window displays in this city of thousand cultures. Wander through these markets and shops, inhale their aromas, discover new flavors, and finally—give in to temptation.

BLACK HOUND / Sophisticated sweets
170 2nd Ave. & 11th St.
Tel.: (212) 979-9505

In a chic, minimalist decor, this pastry maker offers delicious and esthetic honey melts, truffles, crisps, triple chocolate mousse, fruit tarts, blackforests, lemon soufflés, strawberry clouds... Their Zen look and rich flavors will dazzle your dinner guests. Order several days ahead ($19 for a medium-sized cake).

BROADWAY PANHANDLERS / Pots and pans
477 Broome St., between Wooster & Greene St.
Tel.: (212) 966-3434

This Soho shop is a gold mine for Cordon Bleu chefs and apprentice cooks: butcher knives, cake tins, iron skillets, three-layered pots, multi-colored tea-towels, ceramic dishes can all be found here, along with other odd utensils whose functions might have to be explained by the staff. You'll get good value for your money, we certainly did when we outfitted our kitchens.

CHELSEA GARDEN CENTER / Potted plants
321 Bowery St. & 2nd St.
Tel.: (212) 777-4500

Hedges and bushes, wild vines and weeds, orchids and dandelions are all here: the *Garden Center,* located outdoors, is like an overgrown garden. Alongside the many plants are professional garden tools and flower, fruit and vegetable seeds for those who want to exercise their green thumb in the heart of the city. Some people come simply for the fresh air and greenery, and others for advice from the expert employees.

CHELSEA MARKET / Covered market
75 9th Ave. & W. 15th St.
Tel.: (212) 243-5678

Located in the converted century-old Nabisco building, this spacious market is the saving grace of neighborhood residents in search of wholesale-priced vegetables, bread, meat, fish, wine and Italian products. Indispensable professional kitchen utensils from *Bowery Kitchen Supplies* are also available here. The building was redone by architect Jeff

Chapter 6

Vanderberg, combining the atmosphere of a Parisian passageway and an unusual post-industrial gallery, where all the original construction elements—beams, bricks, rusty pipes, slabs of granite, corrugated tin and cement—are exposed and part of the decor.

CUPCAKE CAFE / Birthday cakes
522 9th Ave. & W. 39th St.
Tel.: (212) 465-1530

An unexpected celebration? A last-minute dinner party? Hurry over to the *Cupcake Cafe*, and order one of their made-to-measure party cakes. The size, style—chocolate-layer, strawberry mousse or carrot cake—and decoration is up to you so let your imagination go wild. The pastry chefs at *Cupcake* will create all the flowers, figurines, good wishes or landscapes that you can dream up. When you go back to pick up your masterpiece, don't forget to taste the house doughnuts—they're said to be the best in New York.

DEAN AND DELUCA / Groceries for the stars
560 Broadway & Prince St.
Tel.: (212) 226-6800

Giorgio Deluca wanted to be a history teacher. But this grandson of an Italian immigrant disliked his first years of teaching so much that he went out on his own and opened a cheese store. That was 1973, when Soho was still bohemian and industrial. Twenty-five years later, *Deluca's* luxury grocery store is the preferred supermarket of yuppies, gourmets and nostalgic Europeans. All sorts of imported basic foodstuffs are found here (La Baleine salt, Illy coffee, Cipriani pasta, Mariage Freres teas, Wilkin & Sons marmalades) as well as opulent counters of fresh fish, meat, cheese, pastries, bread and cold cuts. The fruit, vegetable and flower department, right next to the front door, is one of the most beautiful displays of its kind in the city.

E. A. T. / Delux deli
1064 Madison Ave., between 80th & 81st St.
Tel.: (212) 772-0022

Harried businessmen and well-to-do moms from the Upper East Side adore this restaurant-deli with its black-and-white decor, delicious breads and prepared meals that can be eaten on the premises or taken home. The salads are astonishing, the sandwiches tasty, and the prices astronomical ($16 to $24 for an assortment of salads, $5 for a cappuccino), but the clientele couldn't care less. Just next door, *E.A.T. Gifts* (861-2544) is a great address for toys, gift-wrapping paper and tasteful gadgets.

FAIRWAY / *Avalanche of produce*
2328 12th Ave. & W. 132nd St. **Tel.: (212) 234-3883**
2127 Broadway & 74th St. **Tel.: (212) 595-1888**

A favorite spot for uptown residents and other New Yorkers who throng to the immense Fairway in Harlem despite its remote location. It's got mountains of vegetables, mushrooms and dried fruits, cheese and cold cuts all over, coffees and breads, fish and cereals, pasta and dairy products, tea, salads, prepared dishes, herbs and spices—and everything is sparklingly fresh. For meat, fish and other perishables, you enter a gigantic cold storage room after having slipped on one of the shop's jackets. And if you're searching for refinement like caviar and other rarities, you can also head up to *Zabar's* (787-2000) just six blocks north of the Fairway on Broadway, where the food is just as appetizing, but much more expensive.

FLOWER SHOP / *Magical bouquets*
399 Bleecker St. & W. 11th St.
Tel.: (212) 352-1224

This minuscule trove of scent and color offers up rare plants from the ends of the earth: mango-lilies, tulip trees, fiddleheads, Chinese peonies, chocolate cosmos, bunches of miniature bananas and tango roses from Nice. David Browne, the owner, is also a painter and decorator and creates unique and personal bouquets that are works of art. Even if you don't have someone you want to shower in flowers, don't miss his breathtaking and ever-changing window display—it looks like a floral cave from the Arabian Nights.

GOURMET GARAGE / *Fine foods*
453 Broome St. & Mercer St.
Tel.: (212) 941-5850

Less chichi than *Balducci's*, and a lot cheaper than *Dean & Deluca's*, this grocery store (which looks more like a warehouse) is the place where gourmets-in-the-know do their shopping. It's got a profusion of produce and luxury goods, from freshly gathered watercress to home-made raviolis and duck paté, girolle mushrooms, live lobsters and multi-colored peppercorns.

Chapter 6

The take-out counter, which serves up paninis and crisp salads for after-noon cravings, is a delight. Other branches: 301 E. 64th St. (535-6271), Broadway & 96th St. (663-0656), 7th Ave. & 10th St. (699-5980).

KALUSTYAN / *Spice world*
123 Lexington Ave. & 28th St.
Tel.: (212) 685-3451

If you're in search of rare spices and mysterious aromas, head over to this well-known shop of Little India. *Kalustyan* also offers twenty-five kinds of rice: basmati, wild, black rice, gobindovog and wehani among others, as well as a wide variety of grains, nuts and dried herbs. Don't hesitate to look into the neighboring shops, unless you take the trip to Jackson Heights (73rd and 74th St. in Queens), a neighborhood chock full of Indian and Pakistani shops.

KAM MAN SUPERMARKET / *Chinese goodies*
200 Canal St. & Mulberry St.
Tel.: (212) 571-0330

Be ready for anything when you enter this Chinese market, nicknamed the *Zabar's* of Chinatown—from potted roots to dried lychees, green pumpkin juice to sea snakes, freeze-dried barracuda to pickled chicken feet, and pac-kages of seahorses to turtle jelly. There are surprises, and maybe even a dizzy spell, down every aisle. If you're brave, taste the piping-hot fritters offered by the salesgirls. You will also find everything you need to prepare a tantalizing Chinese meal—utensils and classic ingredients like green tea, all sorts of rice, Asian vegetables and glazed meats roasted on the premises.

M&I INTERNATIONAL FOOD / *Russian-Ukrainian food hall*
249 Brighton Beach Ave., between 2nd & 3rd St.
Tel.: (718) 615-1011
Subway: D, Q to Brighton Beach

This is where all the Russian restaurants in Manhattan, as well as the Little Odessa community (Brighton Beach, on the southern tip of Brooklyn) come to load up on traditional foods. Smoked fish and caviar are sold by the pound at bargain prices. In a maze of food piled high, you'll discover Mother Russia's typical specialties: pelmenis (meat raviolis), plov (a beef stew with rice and vegetables), eggplant caviar, bilachs, blintzes and knishes—and if you ask nice-ly, you can even visit the stock rooms and rear kitchen which tells a condensed version of Russian immigration to New York.

MAGNOLIA BAKERY / *Candies and cakes*
401 Bleecker St. & W. 11th St.
Tel.: (212) 462-2572

In a fantastically kitsch, almond-green and candy-pink decor, young apple-cheeked pastry chefs apply finishing touches to the brownies, buns, pies and other old-fashioned desserts that are baked in the back room's ovens. The comforting smells of chocolate, vanilla, honey, roasted nuts and butter will take you straight back to your childhood; you'll be tempted to spend the afternoon here. Choose one of the formica tables, or if it's a nice day, one of the benches outside, and forget your woes and cares with a caramel-drenched cheesecake (our favorite) and a creamy cappuccino.

MURRAY'S CHEESE SHOP / *"Say Cheese!"*
257 Bleecker St. & Cornelia St.
Tel.: (212) 243-3289

Pyramids of Brin d'Amour, Beaufort Alps, peppered goat cheese, piles of stilton, gouda and manchengo—*Murray's Cheese Shop* has without a doubt the biggest selection of cheese in the city. The different varieties (300 to 400) come from all over the world: American farm cheeses, as well as a dazzling assortment of French, Italian, Dutch, German, Danish, Belgian, Spanish and even Irish imports. This pungent shop also stocks all kinds of dairy products, fresh breads, olives and cold cuts that can't be found elsewhere.

RUSS & DAUGHTERS / *Legendary smoked fish*
179 E. Houston St., between Allen & Orchard St.
Tel.: (212) 475-4880

A Jewish institution, *Russ & Daughters* has been selling the same products since it opened in 1914. The Norwegian and Scotch smoked salmon with onions, dill and scallions are reputed to be the best of their kind. A lot of regular customers also come for the herring marinated in red wine, mustard, curry, lemon and ginger. As for the caviar, the owner claims to have the freshest and cheapest in New York.

SUNRISE MART / *Japanese superette*
29 3rd Ave. & E. 9th St.
Tel.: (212) 598-3040

On the second floor of a building in Little Tokyo, this store is Japan in a nutshell. The cashiers don't speak a word of English, the walls at the entrance

Chapter 6

are hung with indecipherable personal ads and the shelves are full of jars, cans and packages whose contents can only be guessed by the pictures on the wrapping. The *Sunrise Mart* is our favorite address for strange and surprising food: seaweed paper, sticky rice, multicolored candies, frozen gyoza and shumai, marinated ginger, black-bean ice cream and fluorescent vitamin drinks, not to mention the Japanese cleaning products, well known for their efficiency.

UNION SQUARE GREENMARKET / *Farmers' delight*
Broadway & 17th St.
Mondays, Wednesdays, Fridays and Saturdays

Four times a week, in summer heat or winter sleet, dozens of neighboring farmers come here to set up magnificent stalls of fresh produce with bouquets of field flowers and organic wines, goat cheese and lobsters, seasonal fruits and home-made jams. There is something here for everyone, and each merchant offers testers. A great place to come to fill your fridge for the week or find the ingredients for a gourmet picnic. Nearly thirty other "greenmarkets," mostly smaller and seasonal, are spread out across the city, including the boroughs. Our neighborhood market in Abingdon Square (West Village) is on Saturdays from May to November with five or six stands. To find the market nearest you, call (212) 477-3220.

OUR DAILY BREAD

New York has never kneaded as much dough as today. For those who can't imagine starting their day without a fresh loaf or a croissant, here's a selection of the best neighborhood bakeries.

BALTHAZAR BAKERY
80 Spring St. & Crosby St.
Tel.: (212) 965-1785
Right next door to the restaurant (see Tables chapter), this tiny bakery with a beautiful old-fashioned decor makes all kinds of French baguettes, boules, ficelles, brioches and croissants the way they are meant to be—with a craftsman's touch.

BLUE RIBBON BAKERY
33 Downing St. & Bedford St.
Tel.: (212) 337-0404
The Boomberg brothers decided to try their hands at bread-making when they discovered an old wood-burning stove in the cellar of their new bistro. Before building a restaurant empire in New York, they'd done their homework at the famous Poilane bakery in France. The ultra-long baguettes, country loaves and rosemary bread, cooked on the premises for the restaurant, are also sold retail.

BOULEY BAKERY
120 W. Broadway & Duane St.
Tel.: (212) 964-2525
The same principle: this chic Tribeca restaurant makes its own breads, cakes and pastries in the kitchen's own ovens.

SULLIVAN STREET BAKERY
73 Sullivan St., between Broome & Spring St.
Tel.: (212) 334-9435
A glass brick storefront and a long industrial counter lend character to this simple bakery and the dozens of breads (baguettes stirato and black pane Pugliese, among others) made from recipes brought back from Italy by the owner, Jim Lahey, are delicious, each one crisper than the last.

FRENCH CULINARY INSTITUTE
462 Broadway & Grand St.
Tél.: (212) 219-3300
As the name indicates, this is a school that trains tomorrow's chefs and bakers. What is less known is that the students homework is sold in the Institute's own bakery and that it is usually excellent.

PAYARD PATISSERIE
1032 Lexington Ave. & 74th St.
Tel.: (212) 717-5252
This uptown French pastry shop is known for its croissants, which New Yorkers claim are the best in town. François Payard's bread is also irreproachable, as are the paninis.

BEST SNACKS IN NEW YORK

Every city has its own particular snack food—Paris has its jambon-beurre, Athens its souvlaki—and New York is no different. Bagels and doughnuts, pastrami and corned beef, frozen yoghurt and iced coffee—the variety of its snacks are a testament to the city's multiple identities. Considered junk food by some and gourmet specialties by others, there is no lack of choice. Here are our favorites.

THE BAGEL: this small bread with a hole in the middle has become the symbol of the Big Apple. The secret to the soft dough with a thin golden crust? The dough is boiled before being baked in the oven. At **Ess-a-Bagel** (359 1st Ave. & 21st St.) and **H & H** (2239 Broadway & 80th St.) the bagels are made the old-fashioned way and are always warm and crunchy. At **Dizzy Izzy's** (408 W. 14th St. & 9th Ave.), open twenty-four hours a day, the variety will astound you (sesame, poppy seed, spinach, onion, garlic, cinnamon, nut, etc.) as will the cream cheese spreads and delicious fillings that range from salmon to chocolate chips.

HAMBURGERS: To sample the real thing, head to the **Corner Bistro** (331 W. 4th St. & Jane St.) a noisy smoke-filled bar famous for its "Bistro Burgers." They are rich and juicy and extremely messy. Meat grilled over a fire, crunchy bacon, melted cheese, lettuce, tomato and pickles piled high in a bun make this five-incher an experience not to be missed.

PIZZA SLICES: For authentic pizza, try **Totonno Pizzeria Napolitano** (1544 2nd Ave. & 80th St.; 1524 Neptune Ave. on Coney Island) and **Patsy Grimaldi's** (19 Old Fulton St. in Brooklyn) which serve real pizza cooked in wood ovens: a thin crunchy bread covered in fresh tomatoes, mozzarella, sweet basil and oregano. Heaven.

ICED COFFEE: In summertime, iced coffee, with or without milk and sugar, becomes an absolute necessity and these days every New Yorker seems to be sipping one through a straw while ambling down the avenues. For a unique experience, we suggest the "Vietnamese Iced Coffee" at **Pho Bang's** (6 Chatham Square, Chinatown). Made with double espresso, sweet concentrated milk, crushed ice and a few secret ingredients, this intense drink will send you to the coffee addict's nirvana.

SOUPS: **Soup Kitchen International** (259 W. 55th St. & Broadway) offers several tasty home-made soups every day: mushroom, beef, bean, vegetable, etc. This place was made famous by the TV series *Seinfeld*, who nicknamed the owner the "Soup Nazi." For a more relaxed atmosphere, try **Daily Soup** (17 E. 17th St. and other locations) where they whip up a dozen delicious soups every day.

OUTDOORS

Outdoors]

If you're only in New York for a few days, you might not feel the need to walk barefoot in the grass, get some fresh air or watch the sun set over the ocean. You didn't come to this explosive metropolis for that, did you? Other than the huge, green, man-made rectangle that's called Central Park, what can New York offer in the way of bucolic countrysides? Well, first of all, New York is never more beautiful than when seen from outside, from afar or from above. You have to distance yourself to really see it. Also, undoubtedly because the natives are so afraid of asphyxiation, they've created decompression zones—a multitude of rustic oases and fairytale-like spaces, ideal for countless outdoor pursuits. Neglecting them would be to neglect some of the best parts of the city.

BROOKLYN BOTANIC GARDEN / Verdant masterpiece
1000 Washington Ave. & Eastern Parkway
Tel.: (718) 622-4433
Subway: 2, 3, 4 to Eastern Parkway/Brooklyn Museum

A floral escape route in the heart of the city, just two steps from the Brooklyn Museum of Art, this botanical garden is a haven for the mind and the spirit. For us, it's a mandatory seasonal pilgrimage. In May we come to see the lilac bushes, the intoxicating rose gardens and the Japanese Art Festival under the blossoming cherry trees. In the fall, we drift through the vibrant tones of yellow, reds and purples as well as the exotic greenhouses. We never forget the Scent Garden just behind the tiny lake. In this bewitchingly delicate circular plantation, geraniums smell like apricots and mutton-feet mushrooms exhale cinnamon and tar. While some of the aromas seem right out of a chemical factory, other flowers will envelop you in new and magical fragrances.

BROOKLYN BRIDGE / A must
Entrance at City Hall

The unavoidable and magnificent Brooklyn Bridge—we implore you to explore it, east and west, up and down, as often as possible. In the morning, take the path toward the sun as it rises over Brooklyn. At dusk, admire the ever-changing silhouettes on the skyscrapers of Wall Street. In the summer, everything shimmers with heat and in winter, the Bridge sparkles. This uniquely New York promenade is worth its weight in gold, and even more so if you tack on a trip to Dumbo (see Arts, Festivals) or Brooklyn Heights. Once in Brooklyn, don't forget to grab a drink at the *River Café*. On the water, under the Bridge, this elegant restaurant offers a gorgeous view of Manhattan's skyline (please note: gentlemen must wear jackets after 6pm).

CENTRAL PARK WILDLIFE CENTER / Zippety zoo
Entrance on 5th Ave. & 64th St.
Tel.: (212) 861-6030
www.wcs.org

A lot of people ignore the fact that, among its myriad treasures, Central Park hides a tiny zoo. To see giraffes, kangaroos and herds of gazelles you'll be better off visiting the Bronx Zoo (we find it a bit depressing), but for penguins, red-bottomed monkeys and polar bears frolicking in ice water for hours, the Central Park Wildlife Center is the place. There's also a mini-zoo for kids, where, in between marvelling at goats, herons and turtles, children spend hours on end wandering through the mazes, miniature grottos and swings.

COMMUNITY GARDENS / *Asphalt green*
Info Green Guerillas: (212) 674-8124
www.greenguerillas.org

One of the things we love most in New York is the surprise of turning a corner and happening upon a patch of green. Although endangered today by the city's real-estate sharks, these community gardens have been sprouting for more than twenty years on empty lots that the neighborhood associations take over. There are two that we particularly like. Planted in 1973, the Liz Christie Garden on the corner of Houston Street and the Bowery was the first of its kind: a mass of flowers, trees and birds, a small vegetable garden and a few rare plants. On the corner of 6th Street and Avenue B, a splendid garden planted around a psychedelic sculpture by Eddie Boros: forty-five feet high and built with materials collected from garbage cans perfectly symbolizes the anarchist spirit of the East Village.

FIRE ISLAND / *A day at the beach*

Leave the asphalt and urban grind behind for a day, and go breathe the sea air on Fire Island. This narrow, half-wild sand bar to the south of Long Island is lined with thirty miles of immaculate beaches on its Atlantic side and a string of tiny villages and pinewoods on its bay side. At the western extremity, the Robert Moses Beach is the easiest to access if you're coming from Manhattan. A natural reserve, it's equipped with showers, a snack bar and some public barbecues, along with plenty of empty stretches of sand and waves. Take the train from Penn Station (33rd St. and 7th Ave.) toward Babylon, then transfer to the bus for Robert Moses (combined ticket $12). Further east, Ocean Beach is a long beach lined with dunes and windswept wooden cottages. If you choose this beach, take the train (again, from Penn Station) toward Bay Shore, then hop on the picturesque little ferry that will drop you off on the island. Follow one of the sandy paths that leads straight to the shoreline. For more information and schedules, contact the Long Island Rail Road (LIRR): 800-649-6969.

HOBOKEN FERRY / *Mini cruise*
Departure from the World Financial Center
Tel.: (800) 533-3779

Forget tourist traps like the Circle Line, Staten Island Ferry and boat ride to the Statue of Liberty, and jump on the ferry boat to Hoboken, New Jersey. You'll be able to admire the New York skyline from a new perspective and spend a few hours in this fun little town. Our pal Lisa, who is always full of good advice, told us about a great Cuban restaurant in Hoboken to which she treks every weekend all the way from Brooklyn: *La Isla*, on Washington St., between 1st and 2nd St.

JAMAICA BAY WILDLIFE REFUGE / *Wilderness within reach*
Broad Channel, Jamaica (on the A subway line)
Tel.: (718) 318-4340
www.nps.gov/gate

"How is it possible?" you'll wonder, when you discover this natural preserve. Most New Yorkers don't know it's there even though it's only one subway stop from Kennedy Airport. After the Howard Beach-JFK stop, the trip suddenly gets more picturesque, as the train glides along a thin strip of land with swamps, water and sea gulls on either side. Get off at Broad Channel, a peninsula built up by the ocean winds and where the first thing that hits you is the smell of iodine and wood fires. Walk north for about fifteen minutes, alongside land-locked boats and houses built on stilts. You'll finally come to the Wildlife Refuge, where birdcalls will welcome you. There are no family picnics or life guards here and the few people you will see are discreet bird watchers. Salt marshes full of wild berry bushes line the path that leads to the sea. On the lower slopes, signs give the names of the resident species: yellow-legged herons, troglodytes, crowned falcons, green frogs. Halfway, before winding back to the forest, the trail suddenly opens on to a magical view of Manhattan. The city rises on the horizon like a distant and geometric mountain chain, hazy and translucent. The vision of the city on a winter evening, basking in the sunset's golden glow and mirrored in pinkish waters, is still with us.

LIBERTY HELICOPTERS / *Bird's-eye view*
W. 30 St. & 12th Ave. (VIP heliport)
Pier 6 & East River (Manhattan Heliport)
Tel.: (212) 487-4777

To understand a city, sometimes you've got to get away from it. With four different routes (the Chrysler Building and Central Park; Wall Street and the Statue of Liberty; all Manhattan; and even a Grand Tour of all five boroughs), Liberty Helicopters will give you a sky-high tour of the skyscrapers. This is even more poetic at night. From $50 to $150 per person.

LOEB BOATHOUSE / *Romantic rowing*
Central Park at 74th St.
Tel.: (212) 517-3623

Did you know that you could row your boat smack in the middle of Manhattan? It's as easy as renting a blue rowboat ($10 per hour) at the Boathouse, a few steps from Bethesda Fountain. The lake isn't huge, but it's full of hideaways where you can take a nap rocked by lapping water, have a picnic in the shade of a weeping willow, or simply watch the ducks. If you don't feel like rowing, you can always have a drink on the lakeside terrace or have lunch at the more sophisticated *Park View* restaurant next door (same telephone number).

PEDICABS / *NYC rickshaws*
Tél.: (212) 766-9222

You might be able to hail one on the street on a nice day. Pedicabs are the city's answer to the rickshaw, and a great means of transportation when the sun is out, you're not in a hurry, and you (literally) want to be carried around. George Bliss, founder of Pedicabs of New York, launched his business three years ago with ten bikes. His aim: turn New York into a safer and more pleasant place to explore. He has personally trained each driver before turning them out onto the streets, and you can be picked up at your door if you reserve in advance. Until midnight weekdays, 2am on weekends. Prices: about $40 an hour, negotiable with each driver.

ROOF GARDEN OF THE MET / *Balcony on Central Park*
5th Ave. & 82nd St.
Tel.: (212) 535-7710
Open from May to November

Exhausted by the number of galleries and multitude of masterpieces, the Metropolitan Museum's visitors often forget the roof. Not just any old roof, either. This is a magnificent terrace, embellished with modern sculptures, where you can catch your breath, drink a cup of coffee, and above all, contemplate a panorama that's worth all the paintings in the Museum: an ocean of green surrounded by a faraway ring of diaphanous skyscrapers. To reach the roof, go to the back of the first floor, turn right, cross through Medieval Art and then the Decorative Arts, and take the elevator facing African Art.

ROOSEVELT ISLAND TRAMWAY / *Hanging out*
Entrance: 2nd Ave. & 60th St.
Tel.: (212) 832-4543

Play Spiderman for the price of a subway token! It's as easy as the Roosevelt Island Tramway. Coming in from Roosevelt to Manhattan, the ride ends with a suspended arrival amidst the midtown skyscrapers. These few seconds of dizziness are pure bliss.

SHAKESPEARE GARDEN / *Secret promenade*
Central Park at 79th St.
www.centralpark.org

Here is one of the best routes for a stroll through Central Park. Enter the park in front of the Museum of Natural History at 79th Street. Follow one of the winding paths that lead to the Swedish chalet and its puppet theater. Climb the faded wooden steps just behind it, and you'll find yourself in the enchanting Shakespeare Garden. Bursting with flowers and bushes, it's worth a stop just to breathe in the aroma of earth and wild herbs. Keep on climbing to discover shade-covered grassy nooks (ideal for a picnic), and further on, the lookout over the open-air Delacorte Theater and its tiny lake, Turtle Pond. As you descend to the lake's edge, veer right and stroll between the green knolls and cedar trees of Cedar Grove before heading back to Fifth Avenue. You'll meet a great many squirrels along the way and probably a few Korean massage artists who will offer to cure what ails you, although the walk should have taken care of that.

SHELTER ISLAND / *Weekend getaway*

To the east of Long Island, and about three hours from Manhattan, aptly-named Shelter Island is a haven of peaceful tranquility. The atmosphere is rustic, cars drive slowly and people seem to smile with ease. Supposedly, this is where the city's shrinks come to relax. The best way to discover the island's natural side, its beaches of gray and white sand, sea shells and the mirror-like ocean is by bike. Mashomack Preserve, the natural park that covers one-third of the island, has lots of bike trails with picture-postcard views of the ocean. The island is well-equipped and a complete brochure is available upon arrival. B&Bs are scattered all over the place. Our favorites were the *House on Chase Creek*, a charming nineteenth century country house (around $100 for a double, tel.: (516) 749-4379) or the family-style Azalea House, located in the middle of the island and a bit cheaper (around $80 for a double, tel.: (516) 749-4252). Bike Rentals: Picozzi's Bike Shop, tel.: (516) 749-0045. Transportation: Sunrise Bus to Greenport, tel.: (800) 527-7709 then the ferry to Shelter Island (516) 749-0139.

SOCRATES PARK / *Sculpture garden*
Intersection of Broadway & Vernon Blvd., Long Island City
Tel.: (718) 956-1819
Subway: N to Broadway, Queens

The City of New York has finally decided to protect this park filled with monumental sculptures that has long been eyed by real estate promoters. This is good news! Since one October afternoon when we spent hours lying in the grass looking up at the passing clouds, we've always loved this spot. Socrates Park is unique, assembled with odds and ends by artist Mark Di Suvero and some of the neighborhood's residents. The soft hills that slope into the East River are dotted with spectacular sculptures made of metal, wood and cement, including an upside-down horse skeleton, rapper silhouettes, giant mobiles that sing in the wind, and the unforgettable kaleidoscope that breaks the Manhattan skyline into a giant jigsaw puzzle.

THE CLOISTERS / *Medieval meanderings*
Fort Tryon Park, 193rd St. & Fort Washington Ave.
Tel.: (212) 923-3700

Imported stone by stone from France to the northern tip of Manhattan Island, the Medieval cloisters that overlook the Hudson River are worth the trip (that you should do by subway, unless you're ready to spend the day in a bus). Once inside, you'll discover the Medieval Art Collection of the Met, and the splendid unicorn tapestries. We particularly love the small gardens where aromatic herbs cultivated in the Middle Ages bloom all spring and summer. In the springtime, the calm is monastic and balmy. We also suggest that you wander through the surrounding Fort Tryon Park, a series of terraces suspended 260 feet above sea-level, from which you will catch a rare view of the wild New Jersey shores.

ODE TO HOUSTON STREET

When you cross Houston Street for the first time, you will probably be put off by this main artery that slices the island of Manhattan in two, from east to west. Long and wide, planted with skeletal trees, bordered by high, blank walls, dirty, noisy, desolate, jammed with cars and people in a hurry to leave, stinking from exhaust fumes and hot asphalt in the summer, it's true: Houston Street isn't especially appealing. That said, we've grown attached to it, and ask that you give this little-loved street a chance. Houston Street doesn't have the chic of Fifth Avenue, nor the brassy pizzazz of Broadway. But it remains deeply urban and typically New York. To enjoy it, you have to pay attention to its details. In the East, under the big clock, you'll find a statue of Lenin saluting the city from the top of a building. A bit further on, across from the Liz Christie Garden, a second-hand dealer pulls his old chairs and painted tin advertisements onto the sidewalk, as if he plans to furnish the street. Next door, a service station is decorated in blinking lights like a miniature Las Vegas. West of Broadway, Houston picks up the rhythm of Angelika moviegoers. And then, a burst of cafés open their wide windows onto the boulevard: in summer, you can sip a cool margarita and believe you're in the country thanks, no doubt, to the space and the wind. And all those huge mural frescoes! Even if most of them are ads, they're still so much more beautiful than a badly glued poster. Finally, at the corner of 6th Avenue, the street narrows, rounds a bend and slips humbly off to finish in the shadows of the Hudson River. Indeed, Houston Street isn't quite to human scale. But that's why it's so different, surprising and exciting. You've just got to walk, look up, down and around and hold your breath.

Working out]

Whether you're in shape or not, physical exercise is part of daily life in New York.

Rollerbladers glide along the pavement, joggers trot through Central Park and gyms praise the cult of the body. Day and night, thousands of New Yorkers huff and puff, sweat and steam on machines lined up in huge storefront windows. Recently though, fitness freaks have discovered alternatives to these muscle factories. Hidden deep in the city's basements and in the upper reaches of its buildings, small specialized clubs are attracting a growing number of athletes looking for a new kick: capoeira, kickboxing, or pilates— from flashy industrial-sized commercial workout complexes to an authentic neighborhood boxing ring, this chapter offers a range of athletic solutions to swim, dance, row, pedal, run or ride your way to health and fitness.

ARCHIE WALKER'S ICE STUDIO / *Secret skating rink*
1034 Lexington Ave., between 73rd & 74th St.
Tel.: (212) 535-0304

In a decor that has remained unchanged for over twenty years, this tiny skating rink hidden on the first floor of a Lexington Avenue building has the seedy charm of an old dance studio. The atmosphere is dark and even a bit dusty, utterly different in spirit from the sparkling ice of the Rockefeller Center and Central Park rinks. Not overly crowded, this is a great place for beginners to take group or individual lessons from qualified teachers or practice during the free two-hour sessions. Great for kids too.

BODY AND SOUL / *Kickboxing fever*
626 Broadway, between Bleecker & Houston St.
Tel.: (212) 460-8244

There's nothing like kickboxing to get rid of stress. As Alice, a friend of ours who's hooked, told us, "it helps you get rid of all the day's frustrations." This exclusive club, located in a Broadway loft, offers ideal conditions: few students, lots of trainers, dozens of jump ropes, punching balls and sand bags that everyone uses the way he (or she) wants. The room resonates like the inside of a drum—leather gloves on sand bags, shoe soles on the wooden floor—while Carlos, barefoot among his students, calls them one-by-one to simulate choreographed combats. $15 for a one-and-a-half-hour session, $45 for a personal trainer.

BROADWAY DANCE CENTER / *Ginger and Fred*
221 W. 57th St. & Broadway
Tel.: (212) 582-9304

In their spare time, legendary music-hall figures come here to teach the rest of us how to sparkle with stardust. In an atmosphere similar to the movie *Fame,* you can take part in a Chet Walker (the Fosse choreographer) jazz course, follow in the footsteps of legendary Frank Hatchett, or learn tap with Savion Glover, who recently renewed the art with his prize-winning show *Bring in the Noise.* In addition to beginners' workshops, these huge studios house voice lessons, pilates sessions and aero-kickboxing. $12 per course, no subscription required.

CHELSEA PIERS / *Sportsland*
Pier 62, 23rd St. & West Side Highway
Tel.: (212) 336-6000
www.chelseapiers.com

Built on the old piers by the same name, *Chelsea Piers* offers almost every-thing that your heart and body could desire: skating rinks, climbing walls, football, volleyball and basketball courts, tracks, kayaks, horseback riding, boxing rings, and one of the most gorgeous pools in the city. Surrounded by the Hudson River, it's open all summer, and offers an exceptional pano-rama of New Jersey from its sun deck (you've got to go through the gym to get there). In addition, there are restaurants, techno bowling, movie stu-dios and a vertical golf course where you slam the golf balls into oblivion from elevated stalls.

CHURCH STREET BOXING GYM / *Raging bull*
25 Park Place, between Church St. & Broadway
Tel.: (212) 571-1333
www.nyboxinggym.com

"This ain't no fancy gym club here," says head trainer Julio Rivera, a small mountain of muscles with an irresistible South American accent. When des-cending the timeworn staircase that leads down to the *Church Street Boxing Gym*, prepare to plunge into a climate of pain and strain. White collars and local yobs come here to mix it up under the gaze of immense charcoal por-traits of famous boxers. If you're a beginner, you won't have to climb into the ring. On the other hand, the cocktail of jump rope, punching balls and shadow boxing will probably have you begging for mercy very rapidly. Mike Tyson fans might even run across their hero here, who often comes to train before his Madison Square Garden fights. Some Friday evenings, the gym organizes matches that draw huge crowds.

CRUNCH FITNESS / *Cool gym*
54 E. 13th, between University Pl. & Broadway
Tel.: (212) 475-2018
www.crunchfitness.com

"No judgments." That's the motto of this club, where you can come and burn off your calories without being watched from all sides. Brushed metal panels, brick walls and brightly colored frescoes lend this place a downtown chic atmosphere. Other than the classic workout machines—some with incor-porated Internet consoles—*Crunch* offers plenty of classes, from strenuous to ludicrous, like "Firefighter Workout" (firemen's training), "Grooveology" (hip-hop dancing) and even "Rebounding," an acrobatics program on individual trampolines. $22 a day, $80 a month. Other addresses: 404 Lafayette & 4th St. (614-0120), 1109 2nd Ave. & 59th St. (758-3434)

DOWNTOWN BOATHOUSE / Paddles and splashes
Pier 26, Hudson River & Hubert St.
Tel.: (212) 966-1852
Open from May 15th to October 15th

If you're not afraid of falling into the dubious waves of the Hudson River, take a run down to the *Downtown Boathouse*. Every weekend, this tiny boat hangar lends out a dozen kayaks (first come, first serve). You can paddle and play in the waves in an enclosed basin, and it's entirely free. A trip on the real river is organized on Saturday and Sunday mornings. But to learn seriously about kayaks and rowing, we suggest the *Manhattan Kayak Company* at Chelsea Piers (Tel.: 336-6068).

DRAGO'S GYMNASIUM / Pilates Kingdom
50 W. 57th St., between 5th & 6th Ave., 6th floor
Tel.: (212) 757-0724

Isabelle Adjani, Kristin Scott Thomas, Sigourney Weaver and Barbet Shroeder can't live without it. Dancers, skaters and many sports pros are hooked. The Pilates method (pronounced peulatis) sculpts muscles with precision without forcing the joints. A few days in New York will give you a chance to try this special type of training under the auspices of its high priestess, Romana Kryzanowska. This sprightly little grandmother learned the art from the master himself, Joseph Pilates, over fifty years ago. The place has retained a bohemian, family atmosphere that will make you feel at home immediately. Private lesson: $60 ($100 with Romana).

HUB STATION / Bike rentals
81 E. 3rd St., between 1st & 2nd Ave.
Tel.: (212) 766-9222

You want to speed along, climb steep slopes, coast down the hills? Sweat, slalom between red lights, or simply idle away the day in a shady park? What you'll need is a bike. *Hub Station*, ironically located next door to the Hell's Angels Headquarters, offers prices that beat the competition: $5 an hour,

$20 a day for a classic bicycle. There is also a selection of tandem bikes (bicycles built for two) at $8 per hour, an easy-ride tricycle, electric and folding bikes. The shop, which is the starting point for the *Pedicabs* (see Outdoors chapter) also sells new and used bikes, starting at $70. Those who prefer uptown can rent bicycles from the *Central Park Boathouse* in the summer (74th St. entrance), but at heftier prices ($8 to $15 an hour).

HUDSON RIVER & EAST RIVER / *Panoramic Jogs*

If you're a fan of the film *Marathon Man*, you can go run ten laps around the fenced-in Central Park reservoir. Counter-clockwise please (those who run in the wrong direction are quickly corrected by the other joggers). But if you prefer less organized and less monotonous trails, where you can walk and run at your own pace, give the banks of the East River and Hudson River a try. On the east side, you'll go through a post-industrial landscape and come upon an exquisite view of the Brooklyn Bridge. On the west side, from the Meat Market down to Battery Park, the view of New Jersey is particularly beautiful at sundown with boats whistling from afar, iodine-laden air, and the sparkling Twin Towers that rise nobly in the dusk.

INTEGRAL YOGA / *Keep your Zen*
227 W. 13th St. & Greenwich Ave.
Tel.: (212) 929-0586
www.integralyogaofnewyork.org

Crowds, noise, smells, chaos and busy schedules—New York can be an exhausting city. *Integral Yoga* is exactly the opposite: soft lights, meditative silence, and the subtle aroma of sandalwood—this Zen temple heels bodies, minds and broken hearts. In the staircase, a bronze Buddha serenely contemplates arrivals. Each carpeted yoga room, kept in semi-darkness with wooden Venetian blinds, is a different color: the Gold Room, the Blue Room, the Green Room. After three salutations to the sun, a series of chants (Ooohmm, Ari Ari Oooohmm) and several breathing exercises led by an instructor with a velvety voice, you'll feel new again ($9 per one-and-a-half-hour session). *Integral Yoga* also has a New Age bookshop, a vitamin store and an organic market where we come regularly to stock up on food and food for thought.

KENSINGTON STABLES / *Horseback heaven*
51 Caton Place, Brooklyn
Tel.: (718) 972-4588
Subway: F to Fort Hamilton Ave., Greenwood Ave. exit.

On a street corner near Prospect Park, these small stables have such a rural atmosphere that it's hard to believe you're only twenty minutes from Manhattan. You'll get a whiff of the friendly odor of manure upon arrival, see a few goats playing in the middle of the street, find ponies nipping at your sleeve and about forty horses looking for a handout. Walker, the owner, will hand you a bunch of carrots to satisfy them. "These stables are old and filthy," says a regular patron while brushing her horse Cheddar, "but that's the way we like them." For $20, you can take a ride with a disillusioned old cowboy named Joel, who will unravel the history of *Kensington Stables* and show you his baby pictures. Nothing better to satisfy a sudden yearning for authenticity.

MERCE CUNNINGHAM / *Modern dance*
55 Bethune St. & Washington St.
Tel.: (212) 691-9751
www.merce.org

No need to be a star to take a lesson from this famous contemporary choreographer. On the last floor of the Westbeth artists residence, the *Merce Cunningham Company* dancers initiate beginners to their master's techniques during the Introduction & Elementary classes ($15 for an hour and a half). The studio is vast, bright and old-fashioned, the view on the neighborhood is fantastic, and the courses utterly exhausting.

METROPOLITAN POOL / *Art Deco piscine*
261 Bedford Ave., between Metropolitan Ave. & N. 1st St., Williamsburg`
Tel.: (718) 599-5707
Subway: L to Bedford Ave.

The prettiest pool in New York is also the cheapest. For $10 a year(!), you get unlimited access to this elegant neoclassic basin built in 1922 by architect Henry Bacon. Backstrokers will appreciate the beauty of the copper ceiling, pierced by a glass roof that floods the room with light. Try to get there in the early morning (from 7 to 9:30am) when it's almost empty. Mondays, Wednesdays and Thursdays, from 10am to noon, the curtains are drawn prudishly for ladies-only sessions.

PAT HALL'S DANCE CLASS / *Tribal rhythms*
Context Studios, 28 Ave. A between 2nd & 3rd St.
Tel.: (212) 505-2702, Info: (718) 390-7431

Warning: Pat Hall's Saturday afternoon African dance classes ($13) are addictive. This astonishing Haitian teacher, who lights incense before starting her classes to put you in the mood, will begin by guiding you through a ritual of slow movements accompanied by the traditional beating of bongo drums. An hour later, the rhythm is frantic, the mirrors are opaque with steam and the room like a sauna. At the end of the lesson—three hours later—the entire class circles the musicians and each student improvises a personal dance. Some of them are in a trance, while others just grind their hips a few times, but everybody keeps time with clapping hands and tapping feet.

SANDRA CAMERON DANCE CENTER / Mambo, *foxtrot cha-cha-cha*
Cooper Square & 5th St.
Tel.: (212) 674-0505
www.cityarts.com/scdc

New York nights are full of excuses to go out dancing—a wild mambo on top of the Twin Towers, a devilish swing on Irving Plaza, a languid tango on the esplanade of Lincoln Center. If you need to brush up on your basics, there's only one place to go: the *Sandra Cameron Dance Center*. Aside from the classics (salsa, tango, rumba, quick-step and paso doble), you can try your hand at a few lesser-known American specialties like the swing, lindy hop or jitterbug on the blond wooden floors of this studio. In theory, you're supposed to sign up for a month of lessons, but you can always participate in the weekend workshops.

NIGHTLIFE

Nightlife]

Although the ghost of *Studio 54* still haunts New York's collective subconscious, the club scene has moved on. Only the hard-core techno-kids and out-of-towners still go to mega-nightclubs. Hallucinations and heavy metal have given way to the languorous glamour of the lounge—an evolution that owes as much to the growing sophistication of the population as to nighttime restrictions put in place by Rudy Giuliani. But if the mayor's conservatism has made the cabaret license (authorizing dancing in public places) something of a Holy Grail, late nights can still be torrid. Just like during Prohibition, forbidden fruit whets the appetites for fun and pleasure and stimulates underground trends. The velvet rope phenomenon—the rope that bars entrance to fashionable places—is often very frustrating, but then all you have to do is avoid the high-traffic nights. The best nights in the city are now Sundays, Tuesdays and Thursdays, and the most in-the-know partiers don't even think about setting foot outside on a weekend.

2SEVEN7 / *Sensual chiaroscuro*
277 Church St., between Franklin & White St.
Tel.: (212) 625-0505

Straight to the point, one of the owners of this restaurant-lounge (a big trend right now) doesn't mince words when talking about his place's underground bar: "The concept of this place is sex." With its winding light-tables and long velvet couches, a menu of aphrodisiacs and murky shadows, 2Seven7 is definitely a very sexy place. This is a perfect spot to talk, flirt and toast your conquests until dawn.

ANGEL'S SHARE / *Fallen angel*
Stuyvesant Square, 9th St. & 3rd Ave.
Tel.: (212) 777-5415

Hidden in back of a Korean-Japanese restaurant on the second floor of a building in Little Tokyo, *Angel's Share* offers a haven to timid lovers and people who want to avoid crowds. The small candlelit bar, decorated with dried flowers, has strict rules hung at the entrance way: no groups larger than four, no standing, whispered conversations only. Nothing to interrupt your sweet nothings and deep sighs.

BAKTUN / *Torrid freezer*
418 W. 14th St., between 9th Ave. & Washington St.
Tel.: (212) 206-1590
www.baktun.com

Like most of the nocturnal places in the Meat Market, *Baktun* is a former meat-locker converted into a hip, underground nightclub. Brick walls, low tables, aluminum chairs and retro-projection panels showing psychedelic cartoons create a post-modern—but not too minimalist—universe. A lot of people come here simply for an after-dinner drink, but others spend the whole night in a daze, listening to experimental and futurist mixes of the best DJs in town.

BAR d'O / *Nights-a-gogo*
34 Downing St. & Bedford St.
Tel.: (212) 627-1580

Off the beaten track, *Bar d'O* blends the quiet atmosphere of a neighborhood bar and the dusky redness of a classy lounge. But beware, this place can undergo a radical personality change, depending on the night of the week. Often empty, and thus a great place to have a quiet drink, it sometimes houses flamboyant drag-queen cabarets behind its closed venetian blinds. Our favorite night: Wednesdays, when DJ Franco, accompanied by a vinyl-clad go-go dancer, mixes music from erotic movies, Italian pop and certain French 60s yéyé refrains. This Nymphomania evening is also a chance to stare unabashedly at the video screen that projects hilarious soft-porn film excerpts from the 60s and 70s.

BARAZA / *Eastern conquest*
133 Ave. C between 8th & 9th St.
Tel.: (212) 539-0811

"A for Adventurous, B for Brave, C for Crazy and D for Dead," went the old New York proverb that described the risk level of Alphabet City's four Avenues. If you judge by the dense crowds of happy people that pack *Baraza* every Saturday evening, this proverb is history. This long, pretty bar, decorated with recycled materials (collages of coins and Barbie dolls stuffed in a brick wall) is anything but cut-throat. Big salad bowls filled with punch line the counter, DJs blare out mambo mixes, and the patrons spill out into the street—where they are begged to talk quietly so as not to wake the neighbors, who have become very gentrified indeed.

BOWERY BALLROOM / *Esthetic concert hall*
6 Delancey Street & Bowery
Tel.: (212) 533-2111

Alternative and sophisticated, the *Bowery Ballroom* is one of the rare concert halls where you can sit down to have a drink far from the madding crowd. Constructed in 1929, this beautiful building became a shoe store, then a rug factory and finally, in 1998, a three-story rock club. The Art-Deco brass railings, vaulted ceiling, half-moon windows and star-struck lampshades lend this place a unique aura. While a crowd of teenagers swooned in front of the stage, we spent a very cozy evening, nestled in one of the alcoves on the mezzanine listening from afar to the funk jazz of Medeski Martin and Wood. The Chemical Brothers, Red Hot Chili Peppers, Lounge Lizards and Fatboy Slim have all played here.

BOWLMOR LANES / *Roll 'em!*
110 University Place, between 12th & 13th St.
Tel.: (212) 255-8188
www.bowlmor.com

The elevator that wheezes its way up to the fourth floor of 110 University Place, slowly passing a wall encrusted with multicolored bowling pins, is aging. As well it should be: since 1938 when this place first opened, it's been carrying everyone from Richard Nixon to the Rolling Stones up and down. Redecorated to look like a 50s drive-in diner, *Bowlmor Lanes* is one of the most unexpected nightspots in Manhattan. Its mythical American atmosphere, sepia photos and brightly colored bar stools will make you forget the neon-lit bowling alleys you're accustomed to. Here, the light is soft and the speakers spill out oldies but goodies: order a cold Budweiser, choose your ball (we recommend the light pink ones for beginners) and let yourself get caught up in the careless joy of the place. Techno bowling on Mondays, with a DJ.

BROOKLYN MOD / *Football and champagne*
271 Adelphi St. & Delkab Ave., Brooklyn
Tel.: (718) 522-1669
Subway: A, C, G to Lafayette Ave.

The night we went to *Brooklyn Mod*, the New York Jets were getting trampled by the Denver Broncos. In this Fort Greene bar, this was a major event. Glued to the TV, a dozen fans wearing oversized Jets jerseys, were howling with rage and disappointment. *Brooklyn Mod* is like that: a great blend of a typical neighborhood joint where everyone knows each other, and a Manhattan style lounge, with small candles, DJs and sexy waitresses. Sports fans mix with the local stars (Spike Lee, Wesley Snipes or Eryka Badu) for parties that can last until 6am. On the second floor, a series of pretty red and blue rooms leads to a large terrace. If you're hungry, the chef from Saint Lucia will whip up a comforting dish of Creole gumbo.

CIEL ROUGE / *A sultry past*
176 7th Ave. & 20th St.
Tel.: (212) 929-5542

Red ceilings and walls, padded booths, flapper frescoes., this discreet Chelsea bar resembles a brothel from the Années Folles. You feel like putting on a flapper dress and dancing the Charleston, and then slamming one of the Madam's sultry cocktails. Mezcalito, Gainsbourg in Love, Save the Planet: the names of these elixirs are as titillating as their taste. Every Tuesday and Thursday, a jazz pianist comes to play, and on Wednesdays, a Russian accordionist accompanies the languorous intoxication of the patrons.

DOUBLE HAPPINESS / *Chinese Mafia*
173 Mott St., between Broome & Grand St.
Tel.: (212) 941-1282

In a dark, deserted street on the edge of Little Italy, this elegant Chinatown lounge hides a somber past: a Prohibition Speakeasy, it became a Mafia-controlled gay bar and eventually was the setting of a bloody gang murder. Renamed after a Chinese ideogram, *Double Happiness* has kept, despite the Chinese decor, a clandestine atmosphere. There are dozens of nooks and crannies to withdraw to sip a Green Tea Martini (vodka, triple sec and green tea) and whisper through the night.

ELBOW ROOM / *Pop karaoke*
144 Bleecker St., between Thompson & La Guardia
Tel.: (212) 979-8434

To live the fifteen minutes of fame promised by Andy Warhol, you only need a small dose of audacity, and to be free on a Wednesday evening. Launched in 1996 by Audrey Bernstein, one of the divas of New York nightlife, the karaoke evenings at the *Elbow Room* draw a large uninhibited crowd. Apprentice rock stars follow real celebrities (Michael Stripe of REM and Fred Schneider from the B-52s are regulars here) on a wide, elevated stage, creating an assembly line of impressive acts under the spotlights. Even if the sound is loud enough to support the meekest of voices, the experience can paralyse you if you're shy. On the other hand, if a one-man show doesn't scare you, go before 10:30pm to be sure that your song is on the program.

FLOAT / *Lounge club*
240 W. 52nd St., between 8th Ave. & Broadway
Tel.: (212) 581-0055

Recently opened in the old *Max's Kansas City*, this club could well become the new temple of New York nightlife. Half classic discotheque—strobe lights and a mesmerized crowd swaying to haunting techno rhythms—and half elegant lounge, *Float* seems to bridge the gap between a chic bar and a megalomaniac nightclub. Soft, ultraviolet rays, snug candlelit corners and designer furniture make this place one of the most esthetically appealing places we've ever seen. But be careful: nothing can be more fleeting than the success of a nightclub, and *Float* could well become another yuppie disco. We'll just have to wait and see.

GALAPAGOS / *Mirages and beer*
70 N. 6th St., between Wythe & Kent Ave., Williamsburg
Tel.: (718) 782-5188
www.billburg.com/ocularis
Subway: L to Bedford Ave.

This old mayonnaise factory standing on the corner of an ill-lit street is the latest hip spot in Brooklyn—both a bar and an innovative performance theater. In the entry, a reflecting pool, smooth as glass, creates an optical illusion that makes the space look twice as big. A foot bridge that runs the length of the water leads to the bar decorated with a mixed Gothic and post-industrial theme: burning candles dot stone walls, high wooden tables look onto an elevated stage with a star-studded curtain. *Galapagos* is home to the Ocularis film festival, as well as concerts, theater and alternative fiestas, where crowds of New Yorkers looking for new sensations push to get in.

GREATEST BAR ON EARTH / *Night-high*
1 World Trade Center & Liberty St., 107th floor
Tel.: (212) 524-7107
www.windowsontheworld.com

An elevator ride that makes your head spin. Spicy, tangy salsa, techno samba and latino rhythms blaring. A spectacular view. Only in New York, the vertical city, can you have an experience like this. Every Wednesday night, DJ Lucien makes the world's highest sky-scraper tremble with his famous Stratolounge evening, and the number of fans keeps growing. This is a must, even if you do have to spar with tourists. Free admission, but don't forget your ID—you'll need it to get in.

HELL / *Infernal bar*
59 Gansevoort St. between Greenwich & Washington St.
Tel.: (212) 727-1666

The red walls of *Hell* lined with photos of celebrities with satanic horns painted on set the tone. Here, any kind of debauchery goes. The cocktails are devilishly good (try the Chocolate Martini, our friend Mike's eternal sin) and you rarely leave the place with a clear head. If we listened to them, our wicked friends would bring us here every night, just for the fun of saying "Let's go to Hell," or "See you in Hell."

Chapter 9

IDLEWILD / *Fasten your seat belts!*
145 E. Houston St. & Eldridge St.
Tel.: (212) 477-5005

Anti-skid floor covering on a long, airplane ramp and concave pale-colored walls lead into this bar. Remind you of something? Welcome to *Idlewild,* the airplane bar (Idlewild is JFK airport's original name). Decorator Eric Rasmussen found chairs, folding tables and the porthole windows of a 1960s jet, and completed the illusion with moleskin panels, chrome cylinder ceilings and blue nylon pleated curtains. The Muzak selection is as kitsch as any airport waiting room, the "stewardesses" are just like the real thing in their tight-fitting uniforms, and the cocktails are so well prepared that you'll quickly "take off."

JOE'S PUB / *Trendy cabaret*
425 Lafayette & Astor Pl.
Tel.: (212) 539-8777
www.publictheater.org

A new annex to the legendary Joseph Papp's Public Theater, *Joe's Pub* is the hippest night spot of the moment. Part cabaret, part club, this new-wave lounge is an intriguing concept with a stunning decor. A must-see: the luminous bar of black zebra stripes which throws a soft halo on faces and creates enticing reflections in the drinks. The velvet couches are deep and sumptuous, and the multi-level space is both modern and sexy. An anecdote: when the club opened, Serge Becker—owner and mastermind of the place—had decorated each table with a small aquarium, an idea which proved to be disastrous: some of his tipsy clients started getting the fish drunk on Martinis!

KAVA LOUNGE / *Saturday night bar*
605 Hudson St. & W. 12th St.
Tel.: (212) 989-7504

Saturday, 11pm. You've visited all the well-known places in town, without having found a seat or even made it to the bar. Before giving up and heading for the first neon-lit and sport-channeled dive in your path, give the *Kava Lounge* a try. In this simple bar with voodoo wall paper and softly lit, small round tables, you're almost sure to find a table and a friendly atmosphere. The music is never deafening and the barman, who doubles as waiter, won't leave you waiting for hours to get served. Believe us: we've spent many a Saturday night here.

KNITTING FACTORY / *Music workshop*
74 Leonard St., between Church & Broadway
Tel.: (212) 219-3055
www.knittingfactory.com

All the known and unknown musicians in New York, punk, jazz, rock and alternative, have played at the *Knitting Factory*. This mythical Tribeca club has one of the largest selections of live music imaginable. Each and every night, groups and DJs take turns on the street-level concert hall, the downstairs bar or the tiny stage of the *Alterknit Theater* next door. Other than the wool patchworks on the walls, the look of the place isn't really anything to write home about. But it doesn't matter, because this is a place you come to listen, not to see. Several times a year, the *Knitting Factory* organizes art festivals, poetry readings and experimental multimedia events.

KUSH / *Casbah bar*
183 Orchard St., between Hudson & Stanton St.
Tel.: (212) 677-7328

We've spent many hours reminiscing by the light of the Moroccan lamps at *Kush*. The Moorish decoration is an invitation to let your mind wander. You'll enjoy leisurely sipping a Sappho (house cocktail of gin, orange liqueur and lemon juice) while the DJ (who seems to be perched in a minaret tower) weaves a spell of middle-eastern trip-hop. If you're in need of a snack, try a bowl of the hearty lentil soup or one of the other North African dishes.

LANSKY LOUNGE / *Clandestine cocktails*
102 Norfolk St., between Delancey & Rivington St.
Tel.: (212) 677-9489

The "cabaret license" law finally put an end to the legendary swing sessions that used to make this old speakeasy shake. But even if the Golden Age of the *Lansky Lounge* has passed, it's still kept its charm. Imagine, on a rundown street, a hidden entrance with only a "Ratner's Soup" sign painted on a brick wall. A metal staircase leads you down a humid alley. Rats stir among the trash cans. Then, a dilapidated door swings open to reveal an elegant lounge, somewhat retro, where you can sip oversized cocktails (Honeymoon, Bugsy or Diplomat, among others) while listening to American crooners. And if you're trying to lose someone, you'll want to know that *Lansky* communicates with a kosher deli—the famous *Ratner's*—from which you can exit unseen onto Delancey Street. Closed on Fridays for Shabat.

LENOX LOUNGE / *Harlem style*
288 Lenox Ave. & 125th St.
Tel.: (212) 427-0253

This is one of the last bastions of the 1930s Harlem Jazz scene. Forget your Gucci outfit and your taste for Bellinis, and come as you are to this club with worn red-velvet booths, old mirrors and sulphurous lighting. On the walls, a collection of fading photographs commemorates the Golden Age of Harlem and its legendary faces: Louis Armstrong, Charlie Parker, Charlie Mingus, Billie Holiday—some of the barflies will assure you that they were personal friends. The *Lenox Lounge* has an open jam session every Monday evening, jazz concerts during the week and a DJ on weekends.

LOT 61 / *Industrial voluptuousness*
550 W. 21st St., between 10th & 11th Ave.
Tel.: (212) 243-6555

This bar's name, about as poetic as the deed to an empty land parcel, gives you an idea what kind of place it is. *Lot 61* is located in a huge warehouse in West Chelsea, and is a major player in the metamorphosis of this previously desolate neighborhood. The lighting, which bathes the three rooms in a kind of artistic, permanent dusk, creates an intimate atmosphere despite the high ceilings. Covered in geometric lines and Bauhaus-style flat colors, the space is furnished with astonishing lacquered-rubber couches that were supposedly found in an insane asylum. Ask the waiter to run through the list of house drinks. They're all delicious, especially the Ginger Cosmopolitan. Don't forget to call before heading over: *Lot 61* has become a favorite for private parties and fashion shows, and the door is often closed to mere mortals.

MATCH / *After the movies*
160 Mercer St., between Houston & Prince St.
Tel.: (212) 343-0020

The perfect spot for a drink after a movie at the *Angelika* (see Arts chapter). Ignore the restaurant and go directly to the basement (open from Wednesday to Saturday). The black iron beams, granite walls and small red lamps give this place a sober, secretive atmosphere. Order cocktails and Americano-Asian tapas such as spring rolls and creamy crab cakes, and get drunk at your leisure while debating the merits of the movie you've just seen.

MOOMBA / *Velvet rope*
133 7th Ave. & Charles St.
Tel.: (212) 989-1414

If you come here hoping to catch a glimpse of Leo or Madonna, it's too late: the stars that used to frequent this place have long since moved on to other locales (see *Joe's Pub* or the *Mercer Kitchen*). But the personnel doesn't seem to have noticed this, and have maintained their aloof attitude. Still, *Moomba's* worth the trip for its decadent cocktails (the house drink is the Moombapolitan, of course), the menu is small but exquisite, and a certain dish of raviolis with foie gras still makes our mouths water. The atmosphere in the upstairs lounge is austere yet comfortable, and you feel very important just being here. And once in a while, you might look around and spot some starlet sitting at the next table.

NEVER / *Decadent sobriety*
245 E. Houston & Norfolk St.
Tel.: (212) 674-7788

Bathed in bluish darkness, this new restaurant-lounge on the Lower East Side is a cross between a dank old dungeon and a padded cell. Hip without being too polished, *Never* invites you to sip one sake after another while nibbling heavenly spiced sushi and maki. Early birds can claim one of the two private alcoves near the entrance. As our friend Mike remarked, "the sense of intimacy is so strong that ten people could be naked, and only the waitress would notice."

PRAVDA / *Russian hideout*
281 Lafayette St., between Houston & Prince St.
Tel.: (212) 226-4944

Pravda isn't really a secret anymore, despite its cave-like atmosphere and hidden entrance, because all New York comes here for "tusovka"—party time. This underground bar filled with leather club chairs, dim lights, Cyrillic writing and pre-Revolutionary frescoes remains one of our favorite night spots. We love its style, its nonchalance, its circular copper bar and endless collection of vodkas. One of us can't resist the Flamingo, a delicate fruit cocktail, and the fried oysters topped with salmon roe; the other swears by the melon vodka and juicy borscht (traditional Russian beet soup).

Chapter 9

S. O. B.'S / *World music*
200 Varick St. & Houston St.
Tel.: (212) 243-4940
www.sobs.com

Every night, this old-fashioned club vibrates with rhythms from all over the world: reggae, bhangra, calypso, salsa, rumba, rai, and the Brazilian beats of the bossa nova, tropicalia and samba are featured every Saturday night (S.O.B. stands for Sounds of Brazil). The decoration is nothing fancy, no one in the crowd was ever on anyone's best-dressed list, but for those who like to dance, alone or in a couple, *S.O.B.'s* is a must. The Day's Special Cocktail is announced on a chalkboard and changes with the evening's nationality: sake for Japanese nights, rum drinks for tropical parties, and of course, Capirinha on Saturdays.

SAPPHIRE / *Get ready to groove*
249 Eldridge St., between Houston & Stanton St.
Tel.: (212) 777-5153

It was in this tiny little club that we pulled our first all-nighter in New York. The *Sapphire* has been the place for over-the-top nights in the city for many years (especially on Sundays and Tuesdays). Although it doesn't look like much with its blue candles, plastic couches and faded red curtains, late at night, the regulars push back tables and chairs and throw themselves into an irresistible dancing frenzy. The music mixes rap and soul, funk and house. Grab a drink at *bOb* next door, and go to the *Sapphire* at about 1am—ready for more drinks and to move and groove until dawn.

SHINE / *Lunatic club*
285 W. Broadway & Canal St.
Tel.: (212) 941-0900
www.shinelive.com

Night club, bar-lounge, concert hall and circus arena, this Tribeca club is a bit of everything rolled into one. "I wanted to make a show palace for the new millenium," explains the young owner, Marcus Linial, while making sure that everyone is having a good time. *Shine's* decor is an eclectic mix of voodoo and kitsch, totem poles and fractal tapestries. Here, you can watch a concert or a stand-up comedian, clowns and other silly perfor-mances ranging from a fire-eater to a chain-saw juggler to a Michael

Jackson impersonator on rollerblades. When nobody's on stage, the gifted DJs take up the space with musical mixes that make the crowd go wild.

SIBERIA / *Underground shots*
Subway station 1/9 (downtown side) Broadway & 50th St.
Tel.: (212) 333-4141

This closet-sized bar is a funny little place hidden in the corner of a subway station. Rumor has it that it used to be a meeting place for KGB agents. With its graffiti-covered walls, broken-down sofa, tipsy pinball machine and dark reddish lighting, *Siberia* looks more like a miniature red-light district than a lair for spies. To get a dose of the seedy East Village without leaving midtown, all you have to do is gulp down a few icy vodkas here. It's even weirder when you resurface at street level, suddenly surrounded by giant poster ads and Disney Towers.

SULLIVAN ST LOUNGE AT LIFE / *Very V.I.P.*
158 Bleecker St. & Thompson St.
Tel.: (212) 420-1999

Strangely enough, this is where we had the idea to write this guidebook—under the influence, of course, but primarily inspired by the exclusive and secretive atmosphere of the place. To get in, you have to cross the main dance floor at *Life*, gain access to the first V.I.P. room (noisy and not very interesting) and leave by the back door that leads into a small, dark corridor. You finally enter a space with brick walls, antique armchairs and moire drapes—the kingdom of nonchalant chic and continuous debauchery. House music and techno fans should choose an evening when the sexy Jackie Christie —most sought after female DJ in the city—is working the turntables.

VERUKA / *Beautiful people*
525 Broome St., between Thompson St. & 6th Ave.
Tel.: (212) 625-1717

In a town where a bar's reputation is measured by the number of times Leonardo Di Caprio has shown up, the current winner is *Veruka*. This ultra-exclusive lounge is the most photographed by the paparazzi-press. And if you're not a V.I.P., you should make sure you look like one to get in, in which case the 5-foot11-inch-waitresses will serve you $12-cocktails in a trendy Fred Schneider decor (the man behind *Moomba*). But beware: we can't promise that this will still be the case after this book is published. *Veruka* is one of those clubs that are made or broken by the whims of the stars.

VOID / *The black hole*
16 Mercer St. & Canal St.
Tel.: (212) 941.6492

You've got to go through the door of a scruffy-looking residential building scrawled with Chinese graffiti to enter this strange bar. On the edge of Soho, at the corner of an empty street, *Void* is a large, dark, bare space. Curtains, lounge chairs, counter, coffee tables—all is black. You almost feel like you've been sent back in time, when Soho was still underground and the trend was for Bauhaus. The only colorful touches: movies projected onto a big screen at the back of the room (call ahead for program information), and the violet-colored sangrias concocted by Laine, the talkative waitress highly in contrast with her surroundings.

ZINC BAR / *Mini Jazz club*
90 Houston St. & La Guardia
Tel.: (212) 477.8337
www.zincbar.com

If you find the prices at the *Village Vanguard* a bit too steep, and the snobs at the *Blue Note* are getting to you, try this tiny underground bar with its zinc ceiling and small round tables. Every evening, you can listen to live jazz, flamenco, African, Latin or Brazilian groups; it's only $5 to get in, and the atmosphere is heady, smoky and overheated. The *Zinc* is purely and simply a typical New York jazz club, the kind you hardly find anymore in the Big Apple.

Chapter 9

UNDERGROUND TURNTABLES
by DJ Shef

It's true—Giuliani's heavy hand has come down hard on the City, and certain purists claim that he crushed New York's underground scene altogether. For all these pessimists, I'd suggest a dose of Soundlab. This association was founded by DJ Spooky and DJ Singe, and brings together a cohort of musical tinkerers, multimedia artists and other artistic agitators that work throughout the boroughs. From the Abstrakt Future Lounge (weekly) to the turntable festivals (DJ competitions), to the visionary Cultural Alchemy parties (musical, visual, choreographic and culinary experiments), their events continuously push the limits of avant-gardism. Illbient, the alchemy of sound that blends hip-hop rhythms, ambient and drum 'n bass is their creation. If London has its Big Beat, Paris its cosmic disco and the southern United States its hip-hop, only New York is able to blend all these sounds together to create something new and unique.
Soundlab infomix: (212) 726-1724

In a more established style, the nights at Organic Grooves are just as vibrant and alternative. Each week, this tribe of DJs led by Sasha Crnobrnja sets the crowds on fire with eclectic, hypnotic rhythms. An amalgam of industrial noise and ethno-tribal beats, funk and folk, along with subliminal blends of trance and urban, the Organic Grooves are also identifiable by the presence of live musicians (flutes, bongos, keyboards) that accompany the DJs. The end result is an uncontrollable rhythmic explosion.
Info: (212) 439-1147, www.codek.com)

COCKTAIL NATION

America became a cocktail nation in the 1950s. After a long dry spell—Prohibition, the Depression and the War—the country woke up with a sudden thirst for shimmering, translucent and amber concoctions. Today's trend towards lounges has helped New York remember these elixirs. You can order a cocktail in any bar, and most bars have their own specialty (ask for a list of the house drinks). Antique shops are full of the long-stemmed Martini glasses and cocktail shakers from the past, and the most humble corner deli sells the indispensable Rose's Lime Juice which is probably the best concentrated juice in the world. So, why not learn how to make them yourself? It certainly gets the party rolling. Here are our recipes:

THE MANHATTAN
The strength and the slightly bitter taste of this old classic (it's said to have been invented in the 1870s) makes it the most masculine of cocktails.

- A measure of whiskey
- 1/3 vermouth
- 1/3 angostura bitters
- 6 ice cubes

Shake all ingredients together, serve over ice with a maraschino cherry in a whiskey glass.

THE COSMOPOLITAN
With such a distinguished name, it was bound to become the favorite cocktail of New York nightlife. This pinkish liquid has already become a bit outdated, but the chic bars have invented all sorts of delicious variations (Tajmapolitan, Moombapolitan, Gingerpolitan, etc.).

- A measure of vodka
- 1/3 triple sec
- 1/8 fresh lemon juice
- 1/8 Rose's Lime Juice
- a drop of cranberry juice
- crushed ice.

Shake with the ice. Strain. Serve with a twist of lime in a Martini glass.

THE BLUE ROOM
This is the cocktail we serve at all our parties, lighting them up with its almost fluorescent blue. Here's Brandon's version:

- A measure of peach vodka
- 1/4 curaçao blue
- 1/8 Rose's Lime Juice
- crushed ice

Shake with the ice. Strain. Serve with a maraschino cherry in a Martini glass.

THE CHOCOLATE MARTINI
This variety of Martini makes a great dessert. This is our friend Garrett's recipe:

- A measure of vanilla-flavored vodka
- 1/3 white creme de cacao
- 1/4 Godiva chocolate liqueur
- crushed ice

Shake with the ice. Strain. Serve with a stick of natural vanilla or cinnamon in a Martini glass, powdered with bitter cocoa.

SERVICES

Services]

Whether it be quality, efficiency or originality, the places we have selected here all have a little something extra. Far from exhaustive, this list is for people with a taste for luxury, who need something urgently or are looking for something very specific. But never forget that New York is by definition a service city, where you can find people who will deliver, clean, rent or repair anything you want.

24-HOUR-A-DAY MESSENGERS

You've got to have an urgent document delivered in less than one hour and in the middle of the night? **Consolidated Delivery & Logistics** (337-1460) messengers will race across Manhattan to pick up and deliver anything twenty-four hours a day, seven days a week. Prices vary according to distance and time of delivery: $8.95 per zone (Manhattan has six zones), $18.95 for large packages, $21 supplement after midnight.

APARTMENT RENTALS

You're planning to be in New York for longer than a week and don't want to spend an arm and a leg paying for a hotel room? Try short or mid-term apartment rentals. **New York Habitat** (255-8018, www.nyhabitat.com) and **Urban Ventures** (594-5650, www.nyurbanventures.com) are two specialized agencies. Sublets (where the resident of the apartment is absent) or shares (where the occupant is present) go from $60 to $200 per day, and are negotiable depending on the length of your stay. Reserve at least one month ahead.

BABYSITTERS

Need a babysitter for the evening, or a nanny for a week? **Pavillion Agency** (889-6609; www.pavillionagency.com), a family organization that New Yorkers have been relying on for more than thirty years, will send you the perfect Mary Poppins after a simple phone call. Ideally, you should call forty-eight hours ahead of time, but you can also try for same-day service. The prices range between $12 and $25 an hour, depending on the service required.

CAR RENTALS

Autorent (412 West St. & Perry St., 206-1777) has one of the best deals in the city: $25 to $35 on weekdays, around $50 on weekends, insurance included. Prices can vary depending on the season. Other locations: 307 E. 11th St. (477-6500); 464 W. 18th St. (206-1900); 415 W. 45th St. (315-1555); 433 E. 76th St. (517-8900). All the way uptown, **Aamcar** (506 W. 181th St., 927-7000; 315 W. 96th St., 222-8500) has a competitive weekly rate, around $270.

Chapter 10

CAR SERVICES AND LIMOS

A comfortable and often more reliable alternative to taxis, car services are frequently used by New Yorkers: **Tel Aviv** (777-7777; 505-0555) will take you to the airport for less than a taxi, or just drive you around the city (two hours minimum—for short jaunts negotiate the price in advance). And if you really want to impress someone for an evening, **Manhattan Limousine** (865-7600) has the limos of your dreams: smoked glass windows, minibars, stereo TVs, etc.: $65 per hour, three-hour minimum, six passengers maximum.

COMPUTER REPAIRS

Memory gone? Keyboard incommunicado? Don't panic! **ABC Computer Repair** (375 5th Ave., 725-3511) will put your PC back on its feet in record time. $55 an hour if you bring it in, $80 for house calls. In a maze of cables and machine pieces, **Tekserve** (155 W. 23rd St., between 6th & 7th Ave., 929-3645) does the same thing for Macintosh, and sells a range of Apple accessories.

DELUXE SHOE REPAIR

Carlos Mesquita, the owner-craftsman of **Shoe Service Plus** (15 W. 55th St., 262-4823) works, among others, for Manolo Blahnik, Gucci, Chanel and Hermés. Specializing in high heels ($25 to repair a pair of Blahnik in twenty-four hours), he is the perfect shoe surgeon, performing all sorts of delicate operations, from new soles to leather dyeing.

ECOLOGICAL DRY CLEANING

If you're wary of chemical residues and toxic vapors, **Ecomat** (140 W. 72nd St., 362-2300) offers natural dry cleaning. Of course, it's a bit more expensive than average ($5 for trousers, $12 for a suit), but it's good for the environment, your personal health and your clothes. Free pick-up and delivery.

FOOD DELIVERY

You can have absolutely anything delivered in New York. Dig through the menus in your neighborhood restaurants, and burritos, dumplings, sushis or tandooris will be at your door within minutes. Our favorites: the **Balthazar Bakery**

(965-1785) which offers a selection of delicious sandwiches and salads, and **Republic** (downtown: 627-7168; uptown: 579-5959), a refined pan-Asian noodle restaurant that delivers all over Manhattan.

LAUNDRY AT HOME

Delivery men from **Midnight Express Cleaners** (921-0111, 800-999-8985) will pick up your dirty laundry at home. As if by magic, it will be returned to you two days later freshly washed and ironed. Price: about $10 for ten pounds (four kilos) except for dry-cleaning.

MASSAGES AT HOME

With a simple phone call, **Healing Hands** (486-5353) will immediately dispatch a pair of expert hands to unknot your muscles and relax your tensions. This mobile unit of qualified masseurs will come to hotel rooms, offices or apartments, and offers a choice among thirteen techniques from Shiatsu to reflexology. $110 per hour.

MONEY EXCHANGE

MTB Bank (75 Rockefeller Plaza, 51st St., between 5th & 6th Ave., 314-9800; Monday to Friday, from 8:30am to 5pm) gives one of the best exchange rates in the city, and has up to fifty foreign currencies available immediately. An indispensable address for jet-setters, globe-trotters and last-minute travelers.

PHOTOGRAPHIC SERVICES

We advise all foreign visitors to have their films developed in New York: the prices are unbeatable, and you often get a second set of pictures for free. **Spectra Photo** does professional developing work in all kinds of formats (around $20 for a double set of 36 pictures, deluxe quality with a white border). Here are a few of the numerous Manhattan addresses: 77 Christopher St. (989-0626), 293 E. 10th St. (529-3636), 336 Columbus Ave. (595-6900).

chic and pricey

trendy

romantic

high-tech

old new york

peace and quiet

Index
Index by theme

strictly business

Index

wall street – chinatown – tribeca

nolita – little italy

chelsea – hell's kitchen – garment district

gramercy – murray hill

Frustrated by not being able to find some of the most exciting places in any existing guide, Stéphanie Chayet said one day to her buddy Camille Labro, "You should write a guide book to New York." "O.K—if you'll do it with me," responded Camille. This short exchange was all is took to start this book, which blends Camille's familiarity with the city with Stephanie's fresh approach. Both journalists, Camille Labro and Stéphanie Chayet have an unquenchable thirst for new places, innovative ideas and unknown treasures hidden in the city. This work is all about the places they love, frequent and recommend to their friends.

© Photo: Andrew Kist

Born in Berkeley, California in 1970 and raised in Vence in southeastern France, Franco-American Camille Labro has lived in New York for over six years. After trying her hand at poetry and radio, she turned to journalism and has been a New York correspondent for French Vogue for four years. Jack-of-all-trades, in love with her city, she writes about culture, fashion, beauty, social issues and current New York trends.

Stephanie Chayet has been a journalist since 1994. Having started her career in radio, she covered fashion and social issues for the French news magazine Le Point. In 1998, she packed her bags and headed for New York—a city she had visited often and loved. At twenty-seven, she now freelances for French Elle, Le Point and Le Figaro, covering all aspects of New York life, from the Wall Street stock market to the city's fashion designers.

acknowledgments

This guide book would not have been possible without the support, advice, endurance and encouragement of Brandon Cox (DJ Shef) and Michael Mancuso. A big thanks as well to Julie Pecheur and Lisa Chernick for their precious collaboration. We are also indebted to Martine and Claude Labro, careful and caring proofers, and to Sumathi Duelle and Garrett Fisher for their enlightened suggestions. And finally, thanks to everyone else who stuck by us, listened to us, advised us and put up with us: Olivier Pascal-Moussellard, François Cusset, Laia Cortes, Gulzada Bafina, Alice Black, Kettye Voltz and Denny Juge.

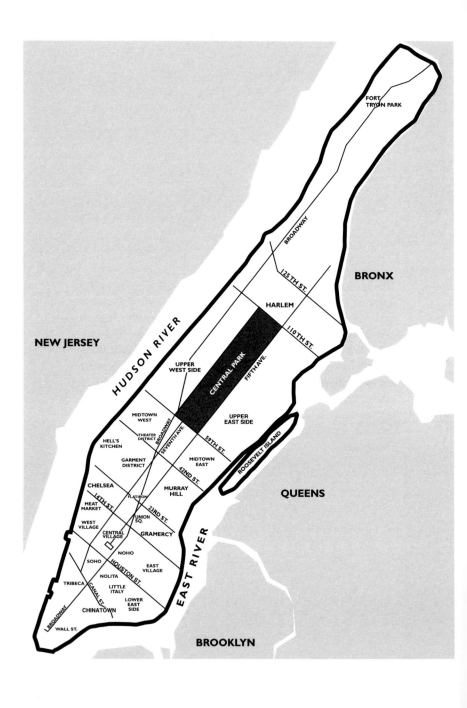